PUB WALKS
—— IN ——
Leicestershire & Rutland

Bryan Waites

COUNTRYSIDE BOOKS
NEWBURY BERKSHIRE

First published 1993
© Bryan Waites 1993

This New Edition 2007

All rights reserved. No reproduction
permitted without the prior permission
of the publisher:

COUNTRYSIDE BOOKS
3 Catherine Road
Newbury, Berkshire

To view our complete range of books,
please visit us at
www.countrysidebooks.co.uk

ISBN 978 1 84674 047 3

Cover picture of Hungarton
supplied by Bill Meadows

Photographs by Beryl Waites
Maps by the author

Designed by Nautilus Design (UK) Ltd
Produced through MRM Associates Ltd., Reading
Typeset by CJWT Solutions, St Helens
Printed by Borcombe SP Ltd., Romsey

Contents

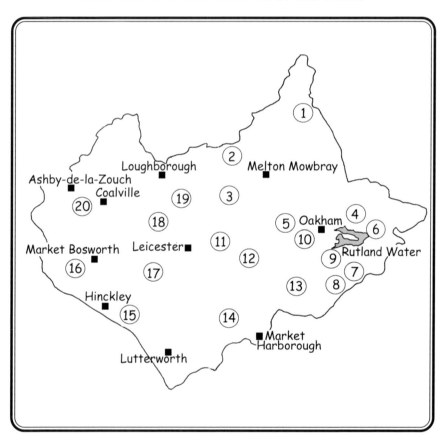

Walk

PUBLISHER'S NOTE

We hope that you obtain considerable enjoyment from this book; great care has been taken in its preparation. However, changes of landlord and actual closures are sadly not uncommon. Likewise, although at the time of publication all routes followed public rights of way or permitted paths, diversion orders can be made and permissions withdrawn.

We cannot of course be held responsible for such diversion orders and any inaccuracies in the text which result from these or any other changes to the routes, nor any damage which might result from walkers trespassing on private property. However, we are anxious that all details covering the walks and the pubs are kept up to date and would therefore welcome information from readers which would be relevant to future editions.

The simple sketch maps that accompany the walks in this book are based on notes made by the author whilst checking out the routes on the ground. However, for the benefit of a proper map, we do recommend that you purchase the relevant Ordnance Survey sheet covering your walk. The Ordnance Survey maps are widely available, especially through booksellers and local newsagents.

INTRODUCTION

Leicestershire and Rutland is, upon investigation, as classic an area for pubs and scenery as the Chilterns, the Cotswolds and the West Country, and, after reading this book and walking the routes, I think you will be amazed at the diversity, interest and secrets revealed.

The selection of 20 walks represents the surprisingly varied countryside of the county that has the city of Leicester at its very centre. The choice caused much heart-searching. As always, there is a tendency for good scenery and good pubs to concentrate, in this case, in the rolling hills of the east and in the Charnwood Forest area. My aim has been to reconcile a good pub and a good walk. Some pubs have been omitted because the rights of way were few or discontinuous around them. Sometimes a really splendid walk lacked a good pub. Often, there was an abundance of riches in one village where several excellent pubs were available but I had to choose only one – invidious!

The walks vary between 2 and 5½ miles and offer a variety of scenery from the Vale of Belvoir to the river Soar floodplain; from Rutland Water to the quarry at Stoney Cove. The length of the walks should suit all the family and they are usually close to other attractions which you might visit during the day, for most of the walks can be done in one session, either morning or afternoon.

Whilst I have made every effort to be accurate, please be ready for changes at the pubs which may lead to new decor, new times, different food. Also, though we mostly know about 'usual' drinking hours, these vary even in the 20 chosen pubs, so look carefully at the entry. Telephone numbers are included so that you can consult the landlord, in advance if you deem it useful and necessary, especially about leaving your car whilst on the walk, or about dogs and children. I have given helpful information about these matters where I can, but it might be wise to double-check.

Even the most accommodating of landlords is unlikely to welcome walkers with muddy boots and wellingtons, so please leave yours outside or change in the car. You should use discretion about eating your own food on the premises even when you buy a drink. Many landlords allow this, but I think they may be reluctant even whilst being co-operative. Why not also buy a snack or even a meal and turn your day into one of real pleasure?

Depending on the season in which you walk you will find variations in terrain, but always be prepared for muddy walks in parts as this is an area of heavy clay, at least in the west, often near watermeadows, along bridleways or across fields. Occasionally, you may have to walk over a ploughed field if that is the right of way, unless you can get round the edge successfully. Remember the Countryside Code at all times, and treat the landscape with respect.

Leicestershire County Council in association with the Countryside Commission launched a 'Waymark 2000 Project' to signpost 3,000 miles of footpaths and public rights of way by the year 2000. This was a big task and I must say, in many miles of walking, there is a great deal still to do. Hence, you will not find all the notices you need and many walks have had to be pioneered. Follow the directions in the book carefully to avoid going astray. There is also a scheme underway to map and clarify bridleways, which should bring results in a few years' time. Additionally, I have been glad to consult the publications of the Leicestershire Footpath Association's *Leicestershire Round*, the helpful books of Heather MacDermid, and the *Leicester Mercury Walks* as well as the numerous local parish walks available.

CAMRA won its fight for real ale as visits to many of these pubs will show. Now it is in a new fight to save the traditional pub and to protect its character, especially those with buildings of historic and architectural value. This campaign was launched as the *Manifesto for Pub Preservation* which calls for customers to be consulted before changes are made. This should help to stem the danger from creeping modernisation which is threatening some pubs of character. In this book you will find real old pubs and I did not hesitate to include the ordinary local on occasions.

The British are not the leading beer drinkers. The Germans drink twice our amount. They also lead in drinking spirits and soft drinks. However, we do excel in milk-drinking. Perhaps it is this combination of milk and beer that makes us inveterate walkers. Don't forget that a pub these days does offer much more than alcohol and basic rolls. You can get all kind of drinks and, often, gourmet food, and accommodation. But why we all go in the end is because 'the inns of England are the best in Europe … when you have lost your inns, drown your empty selves for you will have lost the last of England' (Hilaire Belloc, *This, That and The Other*). Village pubs are an integral part of our countryside heritage and even though they may have lost many local characters and something of their original community, they still open up to us the secrets of the rural world.

I gratefully acknowledge the help that I have received from Beryl Waites, Paul Waites, Andrew Ramshaw and Dr Gillian Dawson.

Bryan Waites

The Manners Arms

THIS IS A TRIANGULAR WALK BETWEEN THREE CONTRASTING VILLAGES – KNIPTON, CROXTON KERRIAL AND BRANSTON-BY-BELVOIR. THERE ARE EXCELLENT VIEWS OVER KNIPTON RESERVOIR AND, BECAUSE MOST PEOPLE TEND TO HEAD FOR NEARBY BELVOIR CASTLE, THIS PARTICULAR AREA IS OFTEN OVERLOOKED. IT IS SECRET AND SPECIAL – YOU SHOULD NOT MISS IT.

———— •●• ————

Knipton, where the walk starts, lies between Belvoir Upper Lake and Knipton Reservoir and most of the village is off the main road. It has been strongly influenced by the Belvoir Estate. Croxton Kerrial (pronounced Crowson) is more compact and the lighter building stone is very different from the brown marlstone used in Branston. Branston-by-Belvoir is situated in a sharply undulating landscape between two streams which, together, produce the river Devon. This flows through Knipton reservoir and Belvoir Upper Lake, eventually reaching the old Grantham canal and carrying on to the Trent.

THE MANNERS ARMS, a 250-year-old former hunting lodge, stands in its own spacious gardens and overlooks the pretty village of Knipton which has the splendid sight of Belvoir Castle on the hill above. Much of the land around is still part of the Duke of Rutland's estate. Once known as the Red House, this property belongs to the Belvoir Estate and has been refurbished by the Duke and Duchess who take an active role in running the pub.

The Manners Arms was a private residence until about 70 years ago. During and after the Second World War, it was used for several purposes and it may be that the ghost of a small child, seen from time to time, dates from this period. As you go through the front door, you have the feeling of entering an elegant country mansion.

Inside, the Beater's bar is comfortable and spacious with a long counter. Exceptional, even inspirational, light bites, salads, sandwiches and hot dishes are available. Examples include braised venison casserole in burgundy, shepherd's pie of king prawns and monkfish, and diced aromatic warm roast duck platter. As for the sweets, they are heaven-sent – try white chocolate and orange bread and butter pudding with rum butterscotch sauce or raspberry and Grand Marnier brûlée with palmier biscuits. Eating and drinking times are: Monday to Friday 11 am to 2.30 pm and 5 pm to 10 pm, Saturday 11 am to 10 pm and Sunday 12 noon to 8 pm. The Redcoats Restaurant is open for evening meals from 7 pm to 10 pm every day.

Real ales include Olde Trip, Druid's Droop and regular guest beers as well as Hardy and Hanson's Cool Smooth Bitter, Dark Smooth, Carling Black Label and Stella Artois. There are

---

How to get there: Knipton is 10 miles north-east of Melton Mowbray and 7 miles south-west of Grantham. From either place take the A607 and turn off at the sign for Knipton.
Parking: There is a large, excellent car park at the Manners Arms.
Length of the walk: 5 miles. Maps: OS Landranger 130 or OS Explorer 247 (GR 828312).

newspapers and magazines in the bar and a specials board above the bar counter. Hunting, shooting and coarse fishing can be arranged and en-suite accommodation is available. There is a garden for children and also a beer garden. Well-behaved dogs are welcome. ✆ 01476 879222.

THE WALK

1 On leaving the **Manners Arms**, turn right onto the road to **Croxton Kerrial**. Walk uphill and, as you reach the top, look back for a good view of **Belvoir Castle**. Soon you walk on level ground and, to your right, you will glimpse the spire of **Branston** church and the village, just over 1 mile away.

2 As you enter **Croxton Kerrial** you pass the church which is on your left. Take some time to look round this interesting village then turn right into **Chapel Lane**. Walk along the lane downhill to the waterworks, which is about ½ mile from the centre of the village. Here the lane changes into a wide farm track whch might be muddy in wet weather. Follow this track as it bears left over the hill. Carry on for ¾ mile until the track reaches the **Branston–Knipton** road. At the road, turn left to follow this pleasant lane into **Branston**. Note the village quarry, now derelict, into the local marlstone, to your right.

3 At **Main Street**, turn right past the **Wheel Inn**, the old school with its bell still intact on the right and, almost opposite, **St Guthlac's** church. Look out for the bridlepath sign on the right and turn into this path between the buildings. This leads to a handgate on the left of a small paddock. Go through this gate crossing a steep-sided valley to a wide wooden gate which you can see high up on the far side. You will need to find the best place to cross the tiny stream in the valley floor. As you follow this route you have fine views of **Knipton** reservoir.

When you reach the gate on the far side of the valley (and it is quite a climb up to it) look to your left to find a handgate only

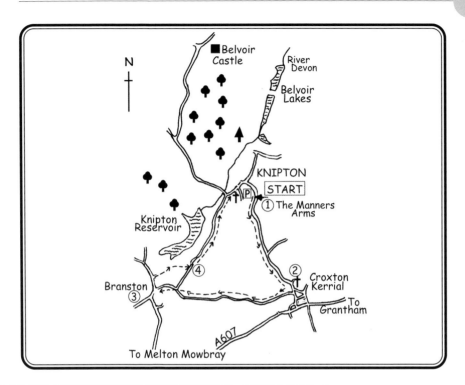

a few yards away. Go through this and follow a large field all the way round its edge until it takes you to the **Branston–Knipton** road at cottages, formerly part of **Croxton Lodge**.

④ Turn left to follow the road into **Knipton**, 1 mile away. At a T-junction you bear right into the village. About ½ mile further on take the **Croxton** road which leads you back to the **Manners Arms**.

PLACE OF INTEREST NEARBY

Belvoir Castle is only 2 miles from Knipton. It is the home of the Duke and Duchess of Rutland and contains a fine collection of paintings and furniture. The gardens are magnificent and the views outstanding. Telephone: 01476 871002.

The Crown Inn

THIS MOST PLEASANT WALK CROSSES THE VILLAGE GREEN AT OLD DALBY, PASSES THE CHURCH AND CLIMBS TO HIGH GROUND ABOVE OLD DALBY WOOD. IT RETURNS THROUGH WOODS AND PARKLAND.

— ●●—

Old Dalby is located between two Roman roads, now the A46 and the B676. It is situated on the edge of the Leicestershire Wolds and the Vale of Belvoir. On the walk you can catch glimpses of the latter beyond Nether Broughton. All around are sharply undulating hills such as Longcliff and Wood's Hill.

THE CROWN INN is surely one of the country's best pubs and unique in its character. It looks like an old farmhouse – at the back is a fine terrace with a lovely garden, roses, fruit trees and tables overlooking a big lawn. A modest door seems to belong to an ordinary house, you hardly dare enter as it is so private.

Once inside, a small bar faces you, and here there is a galaxy of real ales on offer, all of which can be seen in cask form behind the bar. There are rotating guest beers, for example, Adnams and Bateman XXXB, well supported by 20 malt whiskies and many other mouth-watering liquors. Drinking times are 12 noon to 3 pm and 6 pm to 11 pm, Sundays 12 noon to 3 pm and 7 pm to 10.30 pm in this excellent freehouse.

Snacks and meals are available lunchtimes 12 noon to 2.30 pm (not Monday) and evenings from 6.30 to 9.30 pm (not Sunday). They are fresh and home-made and can include such delights as oven-baked tomatoes stuffed with cheese, walnuts and sweetcorn, bumper ploughman's lunches and black pudding and fried apple in a creamy mustard sauce. There are Continental specialities also on offer. Children are welcome but this place, despite its secret location, gets very busy at times.

✆ 01664 823134.

How to get there: Old Dalby is 6 miles north-west of Melton Mowbray. Follow the A6006 out of Melton and, just before reaching the A46, look for signs indicating the village which is 2 miles off to the right at Dalby Wolds. If approaching along the A46 go to Six Hills and turn off as if for Melton but then, on reaching the A6006, follow signs to Old Dalby. Go down Wood's Hill into the village. Carry on past the green and when you come to Longcliff Road turn left into it. Go uphill as the road bears left past houses. Look for Debdale Hill Road on your left and turn into it. This is a narrow road easily missed. Go ahead and to the left of the building in front of you, you will see a narrow entrance to the car park of the Crown.

Parking: The pub car park.

Length of the walk: 2¾ miles. Map: OS Landranger series 129, or OS Explorer 246 (GR 672239).

THE WALK

① Turn right as you come out of the pub door and go through the small wooden gate a few yards away. Close the gate and turn left

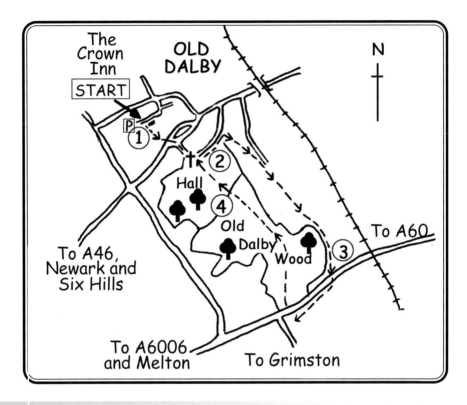

along a narrow pathway. Soon this brings you to the village green. Cross over via a path in front of you to **Church Lane** opposite. There is a seat and bus shelter on the corner here.

As you walk down **Church Lane** you will have a good view of **St John the Baptist church** and to the right a lodge at the entrance to the Hall drive. Follow the lane as it bears left passing a footpath sign on your right. Note the interesting parsonage and **Old Dalby Cottage** on the left. About 200 yards past the church you will find another footpath sign, on your right. Cross the stile here into a path which may be muddy as it crosses a small stream. Go over the narrow concrete bridge and then a fence into a pasture field. Cross to a metal gate opposite. Keep to the left round this field to join a rough farm track where the hedge ends. Continue to a wooden gate at the corner of the field.

There are good views of the **Vale of Belvoir** to the left.

2 If the gate is closed, climb over and turn sharp left along the track, then right uphill noting a railway line to your left. There are good views of **Old Dalby** to your right, also a deep valley containing **Old Dalby Wood**. Carry on and you may see the occasional vehicle ahead plus a house which together mark the line of the **Six Hills** to **Eastwell Road**.

3 At this road turn right for 250 yards until you reach the sign 'Footpath to Old Dalby' on your right leading into **Old Dalby Wood**. Go over the stile to the left of a wooden gate into a wide, rough stone, woodland track. Proceed downhill for some way until you reach three footpath signs on trees to your right which indicate that you must turn into a minor path here.

Soon you cross a narrow concrete bridge over a small stream and at the edge of the wood cross a stile to the right of a small gate and over another concrete bridge, uphill straight ahead to a gate at the far side in a strip of woodland known as **Fishponds Wood**. The gate has 'Footpath' painted on it.

4 Follow the woodland path downhill for 50 yards to a notice 'Beware of the Bull'. I think and believe that this is a deterrent only! Cross the stile into the field and go straight ahead aiming to the right of the Hall. Walk towards a clump of trees which mark the churchyard. You can now see the churchyard wall. Go over to the wall and follow it to reach a gate and step stile in the far corner. Cross into **Church Lane**. Turn left past the church for the village green. Cross it to return to the **Crown** via the narrow path along which you began the walk.

PLACES OF INTEREST NEARBY

Approximately 6 miles to the south, near Melton Mowbray, is **Twinlakes Park**. This is an all-weather fun park, with restaurants, a shop and BBQ area. Telephone: 01664 567777.

The Blue Bell

This walk is an easy journey across the floodplain of the Wreake from Hoby to Rotherby, thence via a gated road to the lost village of Brooksby, depopulated in the late 14th century due perhaps to the Black Death. There are excellent views of the whole valley, of the fringing villages, and each settlement has something of unique value to see.

The river Wreake runs from beyond Melton Mowbray to join the river Soar which then links with the mighty Trent. It is subject to flooding and, in some parts, especially south of Asfordby, gravel quarrying has left large lakes. A series of most interesting and historic villages line each side of the valley, located well above flood levels. These form twin settlements, invariably opposite each other, as they stand in all their beauty on their own river terraces.

THE BLUE BELL is a thatched pub that sits in a splendid Wreake Valley village. Inside there is a very pleasant atmosphere. The genuine warm and friendly welcome makes even a stranger feel at home.

This fine pub is an Everards house with the Old Original, Beacon and Tiger Best Bitter all well kept and supported by Strongbow cider on draught. Drinking times are 11 am to 2.30 pm and 5.30 pm to 11 pm Monday to Friday (closed Monday lunchtime). Open all day Saturday and Sunday.

Home-made meals are available 12 noon to 1.45 pm and 6.30 pm to 9 pm on Tuesdays, Wednesdays, Thursdays, Fridays and Saturdays, plus Sunday lunch (booking preferred). There is a large garden area. Well-behaved dogs are welcome in the garden but not inside. There is a skittle alley and functions room.

☎ 01664 434247

How to get there: Hoby is about 6 miles west of Melton Mowbray. Take the turning off the A607 Leicester–Melton road to Brooksby, and in 1 mile this pleasant country lane will bring you to Hoby. The Blue Bell is idyllically situated opposite the old school and close to the church.

Parking: Excellent parking and easy access to the large pub car park where cars may be left while you walk.

Length of the walk: 3 miles. Map: OS Landranger series 129, or OS Explorer 246 (GR 670175).

THE WALK

1 Go out of the pub and proceed straight ahead going to the left of the old school, now a Field Centre. A sign on the left indicates the path to **Frisby**. Turn left down this path between buildings. Follow a yellow marker post on your right which leads you down to the river. At another marker post cross a bridge and stile, going diagonally left to a marker post on the far side of the field. Look back for a good view of **Hoby** on its river terrace.

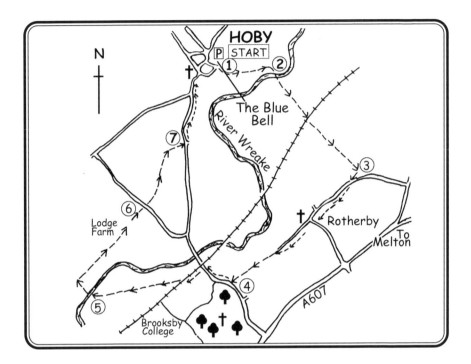

2 Here turn right to a fine bridge over the **river Wreake**, first negotiating double gates. Cross the bridge and go straight ahead across a pasture field to a waymarked plank bridge across a side stream. Then go to a metal gate opposite and by means of the side gates cross the railway line very carefully. Walk straight ahead with the hedge on your right. You will notice signs of ridge and furrow in this area.

3 Turn right at the corner of the field onto a wide farm track leading to the village street. Now turn right again along the street, using the footpath. On the left you can pause at **Rotherby Wildlife Garden,** where there is a natural pond and a seat, plus picnic table, to rest awhile. Look left to see the quaint 'Row', now also modernised but retaining immense charm.

Carry on along the village street to follow the gated lane to **Brooksby,** crossing cattle grids on the way.

(4) On reaching the road, turn right to the level crossing, but just before, turn left through a white gate (usually open) into the college playing fields. Here you may find portable loos and drinking water taps.

Just before reaching the tiny cricket pavilion and scoreboard turn right to find a gate which leads across the railway line. Again, watch carefully as you cross. Go over the stile and then diagonally left towards a step-stile at the far side of the field.

(5) From the step-stile turn right to a brick bridge over the **Wreake**. Make for the yellow marker post opposite, noting the abandoned river channels on your route. Turn sharp right at the post and keep to the left of the field. **Hoby church** is ahead of you, slightly to your left. Cross a stile and make for the left-hand side of **Lodge Farm** ahead. Yellow marker posts again show the route clearly. Go into the farm drive and then to the lane.

(6) At the lane cross directly opposite by a stile into a field. Go across this field to the far side where you then climb a double stile with a plank bridge. Turn immediately left for another stile (yellow marker). Cross into a pasture field making for the church spire ahead and at the far side of this field you see a small bridge, then in front of it a stile just a few yards away. Another stile leads onto the road to **Hoby**.

(7) Turn left to walk the short distance into the village. Note the close cluster of buildings, the cruck construction of some, the Chantry and the church with its Swithland slate tombstones.

PLACE OF INTEREST NEARBY

Melton Mowbray is just 4 miles away. St Mary's church is outstanding and the town park and country park are lovely picnic areas. Telephone the Tourist Information Office for further information: 01664 480992.

The Fox and Hounds

THIS WALK STARTS FROM ONE OF RUTLAND'S PRETTIEST VILLAGES AND CROSSES OPEN COUNTRY WITH WIDE VIEWS. FROM TIME TO TIME, THERE IS EVIDENCE TO THE TRAINED EYE OF THE OLD IRON QUARRYING FORMERLY FOUND IN THIS AREA. IT PROCEEDS TO A FOLLY KNOWN AS FORT HENRY SET ON A BEAUTIFUL LAKESIDE, WITH THE DESERTED MEDIEVAL VILLAGE OF HORN JUST TO THE SOUTH. IT THEN PASSES TUNNELEY WOOD TO JOIN THE VIKING WAY BEFORE RETURNING TO EXTON.

●●●

Exton, with its lovely thatched cottages and green, is part of the Exton Estate of Lord Gainsborough which is now run by his son Viscount Campden. Exton Hall lies away from the main village but both the new hall and the ruins of the old hall can be seen on the walk. Also nearby is the church with its nationally famous monuments. Although cars are banned from much of the estate, it is possible to cross it on foot as there are acknowledged rights of way. Indeed the Viking Way enters from the north and then goes on to Rutland Water and Oakham.

THE FOX AND HOUNDS, a 17th-century former coaching inn, is an impressive feature of the village, standing as it does alongside the green. Inside, its elegance is reinforced by high ceilings, hunting and military prints and a general air of distinction.

There is a traditional bar where pub games such as darts, dominoes, pool and cribbage can be found, and a separate lounge features a large stone fireplace which in winter gives a glow to your thoughts. There is also a 40-seater dining room. The Fox and Hounds is well known for its traditional Sunday lunches of roast beef, pork or lamb and offers an extensive menu every day both at lunchtime and in the evening. Opening times are 11 am to 3 pm and 6 pm to 11 pm on weekdays, and on Sundays 12 noon to 3 pm and 7 pm to 10.30 pm. Children are welcome in eating areas, especially in the pleasant outdoor patio at the rear with its large lawn and rosebeds. This is a freehouse, and guest ales are kept on handpump. En suite accommodation is available.

✆ 01572 812403

> **How to get there:** Exton is 2 miles north of Rutland Water and can be reached via the A606 Oakham–Stamford road.
> **Parking:** There is a car park, as well as ample parking around the village green.
> **Length of the walk:** 4 miles. Map: OS Landranger series 130 or OS Explorer 234 (GR 925113).

THE WALK

1 From the **Fox and Hounds** cross the green to the far corner where you reach **Stamford Road**. Almost opposite you there is **New Field Road**. Go over and walk between the bungalows until you reach a sign on a gate leading into the **Exton Estate**.

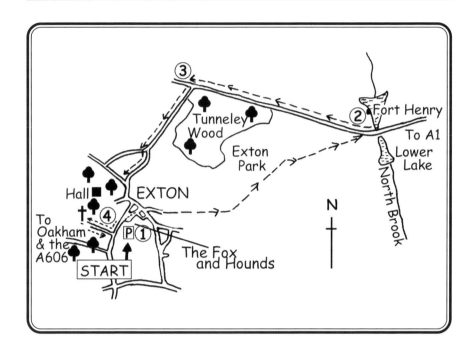

Although private, you have access on foot because this is a right of way. Carry on along this road for about ½ mile when you bear left for another ½ mile until you reach another road crossing yours. Do not go left or right but straight on into the field opposite, where a well-marked grass lane leads to the surfaced road between **Fort Henry Lake** and the **Lower Lake**.

2 You will need to turn into the road on your left but before doing so take a close look at the lovely scene of **Fort Henry** and its lakes. Then return to follow the road mentioned. Carry on for 1 mile and eventually you pass **Tunneley Wood** on your left.

3 When you come to the end of the woodland turn sharp left to join the **Viking Way**. This goes into **Exton**, ¾ mile to the south, passing the cemetery on the way. Remember to take the left fork which you reach just before the cemetery.

You come to a farmyard belonging to the Exton Estate. Turn

left into it via a cattle grid and side gate – there are signs here. Then follow the farm road for a short distance as it bears right into the village. Note **Pudding Bag Lane** on your right at the bend. Once this was the road to **Cottesmore** but when the new hall was built in the 1840s it had to be diverted.

Bear left with a pillared monument on your left (for the village pump) and the old Catholic school (1874-1965) on your right. You are now going down the **High Street** with its charming thatched cottages used as a scene in the film *Little Lord Fauntleroy*. Carry on to pass the village hall on your right and the village green is to your left.

4 Walk on for about 300 yards until you see a sign 'Parish Church' on your left. This points to a lane which you must follow to reach the church. Note on your left the irregularities in the field that indicate part of the old village. To your right you will see the ruins of the old hall, burnt down in 1810, with the original landscaped gardens around it. Further across you will see the new hall, but the best view of this is from behind the churchyard.

Shortly, you reach **St Peter and St Paul's**, described in 1813 as 'the handsomest church in the country', but in 1843 the 14th-century spire was struck by lightning and destroyed for 'several yards downwards'. Fire ensued which caused immense devastation. In 1852-53, J.L. Pearson was commissioned to restore the whole church which was largely rebuilt.

Return down the lane to the main road. Turn left, noting just opposite you **Church Farm House** with a chimney dated 1684. Follow the road back to the green, turning right for the pub.

PLACE OF INTEREST NEARBY

Barnsdale Gardens at The Avenue, Exton, are familiar to millions of TV viewers of BBC Gardeners' World as the home of the late Geoff Hamilton. There are 37 individual gardens, all blending into one 8-acre garden. There is a coffee shop, with free parking. Telephone: 01572 813200.

5 SOMERBY

The Three Crowns Inn

THIS WALK COVERS UNDULATING COUNTRYSIDE SOUTH OF SOMERBY, WITH SOME GATED ROADS AND SOME FIELD WALKING. THE VIEWS ARE ALWAYS EXCELLENT AND, IF YOU WISH, YOU CAN CALL IN AT THE TINY VILLAGE OF OWSTON, EN ROUTE. SOMERBY IS A FINE, LARGE VILLAGE OF BROWN STONE BUILDINGS, WITH SOME OF LEICESTERSHIRE'S RED BRICK TOO. SINCE THE VILLAGE IS SITUATED IN HIGH LEICESTERSHIRE, IT FOLLOWS THAT YOU WILL HAVE EXCELLENT ALL-ROUND VIEWS.

◆◆

THE THREE CROWNS INN is a 15th-century freehouse, situated in the High Street. In winter, the blazing fire enhances the cosy and spacious interior. Hankering for the taste of beer as it was in the good old days? This is the place for you as it still sells the Parish Ales that used to be brewed on the premises and now are made in the next village. When the brewery moved, the inn reverted back to its pre-1991 name, the Three Crowns Inn.

There is a wide selection of beers, lagers, wines and soft drinks at the bar, with tea and coffee always available. The courtyard provides an excellent additional area, with a walled beer garden. Well-behaved dogs are also welcome on leads.

The Three Crowns Inn has a good reputation for delicious, home-cooked food at reasonable prices, from filled rolls and jacket potatoes to roasts and steaks. The omelettes and local sausage, egg and chips are always popular.

There are special deals on during the week: Tuesday and Friday there is a two for one menu and special two-course pensioners' lunches are served Monday, Wednesday and Thursday. Food is available every day, lunchtimes 12 noon to 2 pm and Monday to Thursday evenings from 7 pm to 9 pm, Friday evenings from 6 pm to 9 pm and Sunday evenings from 5 pm to 7.30 pm. The bar is open from 12 noon to 11 pm on Saturday and Sunday, and bed-and-breakfast en suite accommodation is also available.

✆ 01664 454777

How to get there: Somerby is about 5 miles west of Oakham and lies off the main roads but can be reached via Cold Overton (from the A606), Great Dalby (on the B6047), or Knossington. The Three Crowns Inn is easy to find as it is in the long High Street.

Parking: There is excellent parking behind the pub which also has an overflow car park, and there will be no problem with leaving your car while you walk.

Length of the walk: 4 miles. Maps: OS Landranger series 129 and 141 or OS Explorer 246 and 233 (GR 780105).

THE WALK

1 Turn left out of the **Three Crowns Inn** car park, then left again into the main street. Continue until the road takes a sharp right

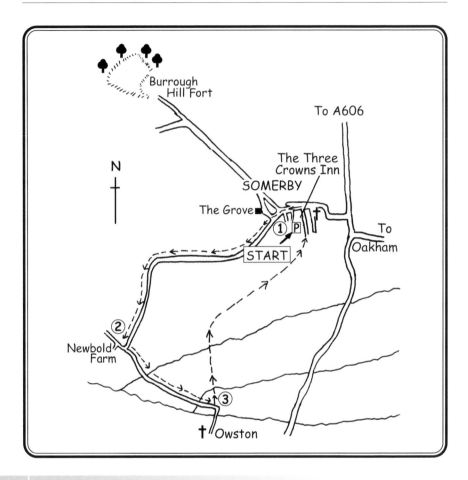

bend. You go into a lane to the left next to **The Grove**. An avenue of trees leads to **Somerby Riding School**. Follow the lane as it bears left. Ignore the bridlepath sign which you pass. There are excellent views of **Burrough on the Hill** village to your right and, in the distance, towards the tiny village of **Owston**.

2 Soon you reach **Newbold Farm** where you turn left through a metal gate into the field road leading to **Owston**. This delightful lane crosses a small stream and then you pass through a metal gate. Around is much ridge and furrow showing that in medieval times this was cultivated land. Eventually you arrive at a signpost on your left indicating 'Leicestershire Round Bridleway to Somerby 1½ miles'. There may also be an additional sign warning of a waymarked deviation. Before you follow this path you may wish to go into **Owston** village which is only just round the corner. There are some charming cottages, lovely gardens, the old manor house and the remains of **Owston Priory**, and the church.

3 Turn left into the path going round the edge of a field, which may be a little rough, until you reach and cross a bridge over a stream. There is an arrow marker here. Carry on to the right-hand side of the next field. At the far corner turn left to follow the field boundary to a yellow marker post. There are good views back towards **Owston** and the spire of **Tilton church** is visible in the distance to the south-west.

Cross a bridge at a marker post and go straight ahead to the left of a hedge, eventually going downhill into a small valley. An arrow points through a gate into an arable field. Go round the edge of the field to the left. After 100 yards cross a side valley via an open wooden gate. Turn right to a metal gate at the corner of the field. An arrow directs you across the field to a wooden gate. Carry on alongside the hedge and power lines. At the far corner of the field go through a small wooden gate (arrow) and follow the hedgerow uphill with power lines ahead. Go through a metal gate (arrow) and keep to the hedge on your left. Aim for a metal gate at the far side. This leads to a green lane into the village which brings you to **Manor Lane**. Turn right to the pub.

PLACE OF INTEREST NEARBY

Burrough Hill Country Park is only 1 mile down the road from Somerby. It is the site of an Iron Age hill fort and one of the highest points in the county. It has a waymarked trail and a toposcope, and is an ideal picnic spot.

The White Horse

T HIS EASY WALK TAKES YOU BELOW THE GREAT EARTH DAM
HOLDING BACK RUTLAND WATER, PAST THE PUMPING STATION
WHICH FILLS THE RESERVOIR FROM THE RIVERS WELLAND AND
NENE TO THE SOUTH. YOU THEN WALK UP THE GREEN SLOPES OF
THE DAM TO ONE END AND HAVE A BRACING STRETCH ALONG THE
CREST OF THE DAM TO THE FAR SIDE. THIS GIVES WONDERFUL VIEWS
BACK TO EMPINGHAM AND ALSO ACROSS MOST OF THIS LARGE
RESERVOIR. IF YOU HAVE TIME THERE IS A SHORT EXTENSION TO SEE
THE CHURCH IN THE WATER AT NORMANTON AND THEN YOU RETURN
VIA BUNKER'S HILL INTO THE VILLAGE TO SEE THE REMARKABLE
CHURCH AND PREBENDARY HOUSE AS YOU STROLL THROUGH THIS
IMPOSING ESTATE VILLAGE BACK TO THE WHITE HORSE.

THE WHITE HORSE, a stone-built inn set in the quiet village of
Empingham in the heart of Rutland's beautiful countryside, is
within easy reach of Rutland Water, England's largest man-made
lake. Originally it was used as the 17th-century court house and

Empingham – *The White Horse*

opposite is the Audit Hall where tenants of Lord Ancaster of Normanton Hall paid their dues. The White Horse is situated at the corner of the village street and the busy Stamford–Oakham road (A606) and by night or day it is most eye-catching and tempting to the passer-by.

The friendly, well-stocked bar with its large cowled fireplace and beamed ceiling offers John Smith's Abbot Ale, Adnam's Best and Ruddles ales as well as a variety of high-quality bar snacks, such as home-made soup, seafood dishes, steaks, main courses, vegetarian, and home-made sweets. In the restaurant there is a choice of wines and excellent food, with Rutland Trout and Rutland Platter being specialities. Children are welcome in the dining areas. A garden for children and a beer garden are very popular. Food is available all day, including afternoon teas from 2.15 pm to 5.45 pm.

Dogs are not welcome in the public parts of the inn but would be able to accompany you whilst you drink at the tables outside. The White Horse is open for drinking on Monday to Saturday 11 am to 11 pm, and on Sunday 11 am to 10.30 pm. Accommodation is available and includes a honeymoon suite with a four-poster bed.
✆ 01780 460221

How to get there: From either Stamford or Oakham follow the A606, and Empingham is about halfway between the towns. You can't miss the White Horse as you turn into the village where it lies facing the main road.
Parking: There is parking for over 50 cars behind the White Horse for patrons and the wide Main Street of the village will easily provide additonal safe parking.
Length of the walk: 3 miles. Map: OS Landranger series 141, or OS Explorer 234 (GR 948086).

THE WALK

1 Cross the busy A606 with great care and go into **Nook Lane** opposite the pub. This charming and quiet lane has some lovely

29

thatched cottages. When you reach the signpost at the end of the lane it signals 'Hereward Way, Rutland Water ¾ mile.' Cross the stile into a pasture field and proceed diagonally left. A notice requires dogs to be on a lead as there are sheep, cattle and horses in these fields. Ahead you will see a very straight skyline. This is the crest of the dam, but it is so well concealed that you would never know.

A clear path marks your route across the field to a stile which leads into another pasture field. Before you cross, look back at the site of **Empingham** with its distinctive church spire. Don't be afraid of the horses in the field. After crossing the stile turn sharp right to follow a wire fence. This leads to another stile, then into woodland via a plank bridge over a small stream. Did you see the moated site and the pumping station?

Your path now follows the edge of the woodland with a wire fence on your left. Beware some thorn bushes and brambles hereabouts. After about 5 minutes you arrive at a wooden stile. The dam crest is even clearer now and you will see cyclists and walkers along the top of it. Cross the stile and go right across the pasture field to a gate and stile opposite.

2 Cross the stile and turn sharp right walking alongside a wire fence and woodland. At the corner of the wood turn left to join the path leading to the dam crest. Turn left again to cross the dam. If you wish you can go down to visit the Tourist Office at the picnic park. Otherwise, climb the stile to walk the dam crest path which is a permissive route provided by Anglian Water.

The dam is ¾ mile long and as you walk along it there are fine views on the left to Empingham and the pumping station whilst to the right you may notice all sorts of activities such as sailing, fishing, and the *Rutland Belle* ferrying people across from **Whitwell Creek** to **Normanton church,** as well as the spire of **Edith Weston church** and the **Hambleton Peninsula.**

When you reach the far side you see the draw off tower which, if necessary, can reduce the water level in the reservoir. Here

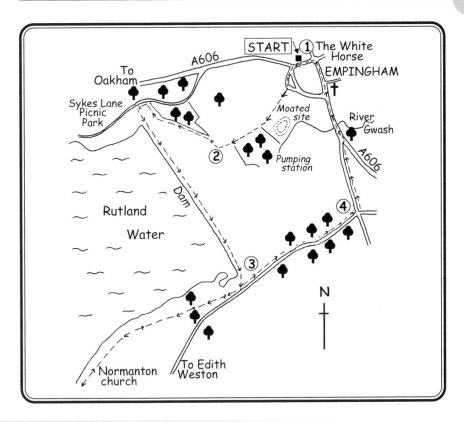

you reach a metal swing gate onto the main road. Look back at the dam and its stone facing before you move off.

3 If you wish, you can now make a short diversion of 1 mile along the south shore of the reservoir to visit **Normanton church** which was saved from the flood in the 1970s largely by voluntary efforts. Close by is the excellent **Normanton Park Hotel** for coffee, etc. This was once the stable block and clock tower of Lord Ancaster's mansion, now demolished. If you take this diversion you return the same way to the metal swing gate.

From the gate, turn left and follow the main road keeping on the wide verge on the left-hand side. In ½ mile you reach the lane signposted to **Empingham**.

4 Turn left at the sign into the lane known as **Bunker's Hill** from where you will see **Empingham** in front of you. Shortly, you reach the A606. Cross very carefully to the far side and walk into **Empingham** crossing the bridge over the **river Gwash** which has now re-emerged from **Rutland Water**. As you look to the left you can see the even crest of the dam but no sign of the reservoir itself. The landscaping has been done so well it is hidden.

Proceed into the village bearing right into **Church Street**. Here you find a village store and an antique shop. Notice the gates to the prebendal manor which you can see better from the churchyard. Certainly go into **St Peter's** which you can approach from **Crockett Lane**. There are many fine buildings and outbuildings as you walk up the street and some modern infilling has been done most successfully.

When you reach the top of the street you are in **Main Street** and you bear left at the signpost (but have a final view back down **Church Street** – it is one of the most outstanding features of Rutland's villagescape). In a few minutes you will be back at the **White Horse**, but don't forget to notice the two working farms nearby, as well as fine stone estate houses with the family crest on them.

PLACES OF INTEREST NEARBY

Rutland Water, on the edge of Empingham, is within walking distance. The nearest picnic park is at Sykes Lane where you will find the Tourist Information Centre, a shop and café. The Whitwell and Barnsdale parks are a little further away but still on the north shore. At the former, you can book a trip on the *Rutland Belle* and also arrange water sports, rock climbing and cycling. Pay and display car parks. Telephone: 01572 653026.

The Exeter Arms

THIS EASY AND MOST PLEASANT WALK EXPLORES THE LOVELY WATERMEADOWS OF THE RIVER WELLAND. IT TRESPASSES INTO NORTHAMPTONSHIRE A LITTLE TO VISIT WAKERLEY WHICH IS CLOSE TO BOTH THE BEAUTIFUL FINESHADE WOODS AND WAKERLEY GREAT WOOD WITH THEIR FOREST TRAILS AND PICNIC SITES. THE RETURN JOURNEY IS PAST THE OLD STATION HOUSE AND THE DISUSED RAILWAY LINE WHICH RAN TO KINGSCLIFFE AND WANSFORD, THEN ACROSS THE MEADOWS BACK TO BARROWDEN. THOMAS COOK, 'FATHER OF MODERN TOURISM' STARTED HIS CAREER IN BARROWDEN IN 1828 AS AN ITINERANT BAPTIST MISSIONARY, AND HE MARRIED IN ST PETER'S CHURCH IN 1833, BEFORE MOVING TO MARKET HARBOROUGH AND ARRANGING THE WORLD'S FIRST PACKAGE TOUR, FROM LEICESTER TO LOUGHBOROUGH, IN 1841.

THE EXETER ARMS is a 17th-century coaching inn which was previously a dairy and parcel post. It lies in an idyllic setting opposite the village green and duck pond, after the true fashion of Olde England. Some years ago the interior was substantially altered and now consists solely of a small bar with a larger room for snacks and meals. You can savour the village scene from the patio.

This freehouse stocks its own beers alongside regularly changing guest beers; plus three other regularly changing guest real ales and a cask-conditioned cider during the summer months. Drinking times are: weekdays 12 noon to 2.30 pm and 6 pm to 11 pm, Sundays 12 noon to 2.30 pm and 7 pm to 10.30 pm (closed Monday lunchtime).

Excellent food is available, usually between 12 noon to 2 pm and 7 pm to 9 pm every day except all day Monday and Sunday evening. ✆ 01572 747247

How to get there: Barrowden is about ½ mile from the A47, 16 miles west of Peterborough and 7 miles south-west of Stamford. It lies on the boundary between Rutland and Northamptonshire, marked by the river Welland, and you can also approach from the A43, turning off at Wakerley Woods. **Parking:** The pub car park is at the rear and street parking (with discretion) is also possible.
Length of the walk: 2½ miles. Map: OS Landranger 141 or OS Explorer 234 (GR 947001).

THE WALK

1 As you leave the **Exeter Arms,** go left past the great horse chestnut tree, the seat and the shelter to the main street. Follow this until you come to **Mill Lane,** a no through road. Bear right down the lane and at a footpath sign continue to bear right. This leads you into a tree-lined track past a stagnant pool, probably the old mill pond. Skirt around the pond eventually turning right to cross a footbridge over the **river Welland**. Go through a gate

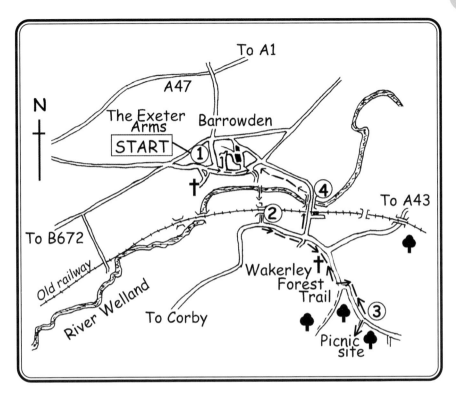

into a pasture field. You are now on the floodplain of the river. Go across the field to a line of trees opposite which marks the line of a disused railway. Pass through a wooden gate under a railway bridge and proceed uphill to a farmhouse on your left.

2 At the road turn left along the village street of **Wakerley**. There are some very fine stone houses and cottages to be seen. Carry on past **Exeter House** which is on your right.

Continue to the **church of St John the Baptist** on the road to Fineshade. This has a very well-kept churchyard and the church itself is most impressive, being now maintained by the Redundant Churches Fund. If you care to carry on for only 500 yards you will come to the picnic site, toilets and trails in Wakerley Wood.

3 Return to **Wakerley** village noting an excellent converted farmyard on your right at the corner, opposite the old rectory now **Keepers Cottage**. At **Exeter House** turn right down the lane signposted 'Barrowden ¾ mile'. Shortly, you see on your right the former railway station. Note that the old bridge has gone and just beyond you see the sign 'Rutland'.

4 Cross the river bridge and look both left and right at the lovely river meadows and the gently flowing stream. Then find the footpath sign pointing towards **Barrowden**, with the church visible in the distance. Cross the stile into the field and go diagonally right to the end of a line of trees, crossing a plank bridge on the way. Now bear diagonally right following the power lines to reach a gate in a hedge into a paddock. Go across to the left corner. Turn left to a gate and follow the path round to another gate on your left. This leads back to **Mill Lane**, your starting point.

Make your way back to the village duck pond but instead of going straight on to the **Exeter Arms**, go down the lovely lane to **St Peter's church** passing **Pepperday Cottage** and **Carey's House**. Ponder for a while in the church and churchyard and then return for your drink.

PLACE OF INTEREST NEARBY

The fine, stone town of **Stamford** is about 7 miles to the east. Lovely churches, a good museum, riverside walks and interesting shops, Stamford has something for everyone. Burghley House, an outstanding Elizabethan mansion, is on the edge of the town. Telephone: 01780 752451.

The Old White Hart

THE WALK FOLLOWS THE FIELD PATH TO SEATON, PASSING CLOSE TO PRESTLEY HILL AND THE BARROWS, WITH LOVELY VIEWS OF BOTH VILLAGES. THEN A COUNTRY LANE TAKES YOU INTO THE WELLAND VALLEY, WITH A SHORT PAUSE TO SEE THORPE BY WATER. FROM HERE ANOTHER PLEASANT COUNTRY LANE RETURNS YOU TO THE SOUTHERN END OF THE VILLAGE.

———— ●●● ————

'Long' Lyddington is one of Rutland's most beautiful and interesting villages. Next to the church in Lyddington is the **Bede House**, once part of the palace of the bishops of Lincoln and later converted to an almshouse. On the village green is the stump of a cross, a reminder that in medieval times the village was a market centre, vying with Uppingham.

THE OLD WHITE HART is a real country pub with a small bar, a medium-sized lounge and three restaurants. There is a strong emphasis on fresh, home-cooked food which matches the season. The new style menu changes every two months. There is home-made sausage and mash, fresh Grimsby haddock deep fried in crisp batter, roast of the day with fresh vegetables and all the trimmings on Sundays, half a crispy duck, rack of English lamb, and much more. These are well supported by fresh vegetables, side orders and home-made puddings, plus a vegetarian specials board. Light lunches are equally varied and tasty at a reasonable price. The full à la carte menu is available from 12 noon to 2 pm and 7 pm to 10 pm every day (not Sunday evening).

This freehouse has Greene King IPA, Marston's Pedigree Bitter and Abbot Ale. Drinking times are 12 noon to 3 pm and 6.30 pm to 11 pm except Sunday evening 7 pm to 10.30 pm. Since the pub is so accessible to Uppingham and Corby it soon gets busy, even on weekdays, in season. Petanque is played most evenings during the summer.

✆ 01572 821703 (bookings for the restaurants advisable)

How to get there: Lyddington is just off the A6003 between Uppingham and Corby, Northamptonshire. It is nearer Uppingham, being only about 2 miles south-east. The village is approached via pleasant country lanes and the Old White Hart is opposite the village green.

Parking: There is a large, attractive, excellent car park at the pub, and you can leave your car there while you go on your walk.

Length of the walk: 4¾ miles. Map: OS Landranger series 141 or OS Explorer 234 (GR 875970).

THE WALK

1 From the **Old White Hart** cross over the green to footpath signs near the swings. Do not go down **Bluecoat Lane** but carry

LYDDINGTON – *The Old White Hart*

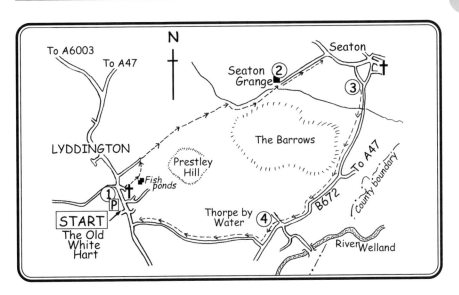

straight on between a house and cottage in front of you. A sign points the way. Notice to your right the views of the church and the **Bede House**. You come to a stile. Cross over and then keep to the hedge on your left. You will see lots of humps and bumps in the field. Look carefully and they will appear to form a series of rectangles. These were the fishponds or stews attached to the Bishop of Lincoln's palace, now the Bede House.

Turn left through a gap in the hedge into a wide green way with the village football pitch in the field on your left. In about 100 yards cross a stile, slightly overgrown, onto a farm track which may be muddy. Turn right and cross a stile into rough pasture. Follow the hedge uphill to the far left corner where you cross another stile into a large arable field.

Again, follow the hedge through the field looking back for excellent views of **Lyddington**. To your right is **Prestley Hill**. At the corner of the field turn right for about 40 yards then go through a gap in the hedge leading to a track to **Seaton**, which you can see in the distance. There is a ditch to your left and you are in a very large arable field, perhaps an example of hedge-loss or prairie farming. Continue to bear right round the perimeter of the field on a wide grassy track. Bear left round a large willow tree and as you walk along you have a line of ash trees to your left.

② You reach **Seaton Grange Farm** with a metal gate and stile to cross into a metalled farm track leading to **Seaton**. Note a line of poplars to your left and, in the distance, views of the **Harringworth Viaduct** over the **Welland valley**. At the main street turn right passing the village sign and lovely walls invaded by all manner of plants. Houses on the left have 1881 datestones. If you have time you could explore **Seaton** and look in **All Hallows church**.

③ To continue your walk you need to turn right into **Moles Lane** and follow it down into the **Welland valley**. As you walk along this sunken lane remember to look back at **Seaton** sitting on its hill. Continue downhill bearing right along the lane until you reach the main Morcott–Caldecott road, the B672. Turn right for ½ mile and, though this road is fairly quiet, take care as there will be vehicles coming round the bends. Soon you reach the sign indicating **Thorpe by Water** to your left. Go into this little village which is so close to the **Welland,** a danger spot in time of floods.

④ When you are ready to proceed, return to the main road and turn left for ¼ mile until you reach a lane leading to **Lyddington**. Turn right into this narrow country lane and in 1 mile, with some uphill walking but great views towards **Rockingham Castle** and its scarp overlooking the **Welland valley**, you arrive back in **Lyddington,** and turn right to return to the inn.

PLACE OF INTEREST NEARBY

A few miles south is **Rockingham Castle**, built by William the Conqueror. A royal residence for 450 years and a family home for the last 450 years, it is well worth a visit. Telephone: 01536 770240.

WING

The King's Arms

THE WALK IS OVER THE FIELDS, CROSSING A RAILWAY LINE AND THE RIVER CHATER THENCE NORTHWARDS TOWARDS THE LYNDON NATURE RESERVE, BUT BEFORE REACHING THAT THE ROUTE FOLLOWS A PLEASANT COUNTRY LANE TO THE VILLAGE OF LYNDON WITH ITS IMPRESSIVE HALL AND FINE CHURCH FORMING A PICTURE-POSTCARD SCENE. THE RETURN IS THROUGH QUIET FIELDS AND WOODLAND WHERE THE REST OF THE WORLD SEEMS FAR AWAY AND ONE CAN PAUSE FOR A PHILOSOPHICAL THOUGHT ALONG THIS PASTORAL ROUTE.

———————————●●●———————————

Wing is situated on a ridge above the river Chater. Not far away to the north, lies Rutland Water. The village must be considered logical in its layout with a Top, Bottom and Middle Street. It is famous for its Turf Maze, one of the few in England. Opposite to this the Wing Treatment Works purifies the water supplies from Rutland Water before distribution over a wide area. There are many attractive stone houses and lovely gardens, some dating from the 17th century. Lyndon Hall was the home of Thomas Barker, 'Father of English Meteorology', who in the 18th century, kept records for more than 60 years. The journals of the squire are now a wonderful record of nature, the countryside and the weather 200 years ago.

THE KING'S ARMS is a lovely stone-built pub dating from the early 17th century and it extends at right angles to the village street. The old village bakehouse is opposite the main pub building and between the two is a lane leading to the car park. There are tables outside. Inside you find a real Rutland atmosphere with a winter fire, a cosy bar and lounge, plus a distinguished restaurant. People come from far and wide to eat here. There is a wide choice of home-cooked food with the emphasis on fresh produce and local dishes. The specials board is always a welcome sight to the visitor. Food is served from 12 noon to 2.30 pm and 6 pm to 9 pm every day both in the bar and restaurant.

This is a freehouse and features many popular and unusual real ales. Drinking times are 12 noon to 3 pm (or longer if customers are numerous) and 6.30 pm to 11 pm; Sundays from 12 noon to 3 pm. In the summer months it is open all day Saturday and Sunday. There is a most busy and lively atmosphere in this well-frequented and popular pub. En suite accommodation is available and there are special rates for walkers at certain times of the year. Sorry, no pets.

This is a good base for Rutland Water and don't forget the maze nearby.

℡ 01572 737634

How to get there: Wing lies between Oakham and Uppingham. Take the A6003 linking both places and turn off at Preston. Wing is signposted 1½ miles from the A6003.
Parking: There is a large car park at the King's Arms and also street parking is available.
Length of the walk: 4 miles. Map: OS Landranger 141 or OS Explorer 234 (GR 892029).

THE WALK

1 Go down **Church Street** until you reach the northern extremity of the village. Here you find a footpath sign and a metal gate. Go into the field, closing the gate behind you and make for the hedge to your right. Follow this until you reach a hunting gate and plank bridge near to a large ash tree. Cross the ditch here and turn sharp left then right, parallel with the railway line. This is the **Birmingham–Peterborough line** and is quite busy. Follow the broken down fence which is on your left until you reach a rail crossing point in about 100 yards. Looking back you have fine views of **Wing** on its ridge.

If the crossing gates are locked you will need to climb over –

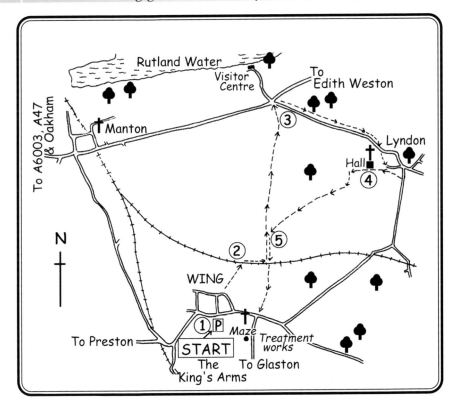

but this is a permissible crossing point. Take care and look in both directions.

② Turn right along the edge of an arable field following a wire fence still keeping parallel with the railway line – you are now on the opposite side of the line. In 5 minutes or so you reach another set of crossing gates and the junction of two farm tracks. Turn left along the hedge line to follow a broad and well-defined track which is, in fact, a bridleway. **Manton** comes into view to the north-west. Soon you cross a bridge over the **river Chater**. Carry on, keeping the hedge to your right as you go uphill. Pause at a gap into a field to look back at **Wing** and its church. Proceed along the path straight ahead with a small wood to your right. The route is very clear. You then reach the main **Manton–Edith Weston road**. Opposite you see notices to the **Lyndon Nature Reserve**.

③ Turn right to **Lyndon** which is signposted, via an avenue of oaks and ashes. Note the lovely pond on your right at a stone bridge near **Lyndon Wood**.

To your left you may see **Lyndon Top Hall**, but soon you arrive at one of Rutland's prettiest scenes. **Lyndon Hall** with its fine clock tower is down a drive to your right. A little further on is **St Martin's church**. Turn right to visit the church. At the same time look through the arch to get a glimpse of the Hall. Can you find the tombstone of William Whiston – 18th-century mathematician, philosopher and divine, and father-in-law of Thomas Barker? It is propped up next to the wall. Nobody has yet found the tombstone of the 'Father of English Meteorology', who was also the brother-in-law of the famous naturalist Gilbert White of Selborne, Hampshire.

Now look for a small gate in a wall – you have to retrace your steps to find it. Go through into a secret garden and follow the walk quietly until you reach another gate. Go through this into **Post Office Lane** in the village. Here you see old houses and also some modern houses built in the old style using stone. At the crossroads turn right for 200 yards and look for a footpath sign on your right. Go into the field as indicated, keeping to the edge of the field bearing right. The **Chater valley** and **Wing** come into view to your left.

4 You soon pass in front of **Lyndon Hall**. Once the village street ran here but the squire altered it so that he had more privacy. Follow the edge of the wood bearing left downhill. You come to a marker post and hunting gate. The arrow points left as you proceed through the wood. Once through this small and narrow wood turn left again to follow the edge of the wood. Shortly, another marker post directs you right along a hedge. Turn left again at the next marker post, about 5 minutes away, and walk downhill to the **river Chater**, bearing right following the hedge line and eventually passing a poplar plantation.

5 At the corner of the field turn left through the plantation then bear right to cross a plank bridge and join the main farm track at the bridge over the **Chater** which you crossed earlier on the walk. Cross the bridge making for the railway level-crossing straight ahead. Cross the line carefully via metal gates then go uphill along the bridleway to the village street. On reaching the main road turn right for the **King's Arms** just beyond the church. You may wish to see the **Turf Maze** and if so you can take a short 200 yard diversion to the left to do so.

PLACE OF INTEREST NEARBY

Normanton Picnic Park at Rutland Water is a few miles north. Boat and cycle hire is available and there is a café and Harbour restaurant. Visit the Water Museum in the former church on the edge of the reservoir.

The Old Plough

THIS ROUTE FROM THE VILLAGE OF BRAUNSTON TAKES YOU THROUGH WHAT WAS FORMERLY THE ROYAL FOREST OF LEIGHFIELD. NOW THE ONLY REMNANTS ARE IN THE VERY OLD HEDGEROWS AND ANCIENT WOODLAND LIKE PRIOR'S COPPICE. THIS WAS THE FRONTIER BETWEEN RUTLAND AND LEICESTERSHIRE AND YOU WILL WALK ALONG PART OF THE BOUNDARY. THERE ARE GOOD ALL-ROUND VIEWS, ESPECIALLY BACK TOWARDS BRAUNSTON.

❦

THE OLD PLOUGH is very well placed, being only 2 miles away from Oakham. The pub presents a very welcoming face to road travellers at the bend in the busy main road. Inside is a through bar, with a beamed ceiling, brasses, and hunting prints as well as a Poacher's Survival Kit on the wall to add to the atmosphere. Reputedly the largest horseshoe in Rutland makes a fine entrance to the attractive garden where you can sit with the family for your drink, snacks or meals. Food is available seven days a week from 12 noon to 2.30 pm and 6 pm to 10 pm (9 pm Sundays).

The Old Plough is renowned for its excellent menus. Some of the famous specials are home-made steak and kidney pie cooked in Guinness, fresh salmon with prawns wrapped in filo pastry served on a fish yoghurt sauce, and, of course, 'Plough Crusty', really large home-baked granary rolls with a choice of fillings.

This is a freehouse where Cooking Beer, Triple B and 10/50 feature (Rutland bitters from the Grainstore Brewery) and cider on draught. Children are welcome for meals in the conservatory dining room and in the garden. Dogs may join you away from the food areas.
☎ 01572 722714

How to get there: Braunston is 2 miles from Oakham on the Tilton (Leicester) road. The Old Plough is on the corner.
Parking: There is good parking at the Old Plough but make sure you are using the facilities. If you plan to walk first, please go in to ask the landlord about parking. There is street parking in the village.
Length of the walk: 3¾ miles. Map: OS Landranger series 141 or OS Explorer 234 (GR 835069).

THE WALK

1 Turn left on leaving the **Old Plough** down the village street to the church about five minutes away. **All Saints** is situated above the **river Gwash** on a slight eminence. Go into the churchyard via the main signposted pathway.

2 Climb over the wooden fence and cross the pasture field to a metal gate opposite. At the sign, go through into the ridge and furrow field and cross to the far right-hand corner. Now cross fences and a plank bridge over a tiny side stream, following the hedge line, keeping it on your right. Here you will notice a small but deep river valley to your left which is the **river Gwash**.

3 Look for an overgrown fence and footbridge in the corner of the field. Cross it and you see a sign on the far side. Bear left towards an ash tree but before reaching it turn right along the course of a small stream. In 150 yards your path continues between two hedges with the stream and hedge to your left. Go through a gate opening and carry on with the hedge and stream still to your left. When you reach the corner of the field cross a wooden fence into a pasture. Cross to a metal gate opposite. At the gate, note a house to your right, **South Lodge Farm**. Go over or through the gate onto rough ground still following the stream on your left. Cross over a farm track and continue ahead into and across a pasture field. At the far top corner of this field you will find a gap. Go through this gap into the field then bear diagonally across downhill to find a bridge and gates which take you over the stream.

4 Now cross the field making for a stunted ash tree at the top of the hill. Follow the hedge to the far corner of the field and under

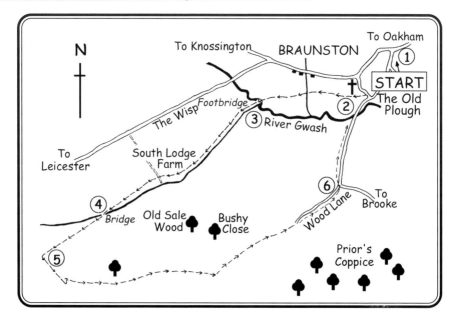

a large ash tree cross over a wooden fence into a large arable field. Look opposite to the far side of the field to find a bend in the hedgeline then cross the field to the left of this bend looking for a gap leading onto a bridlepath. Now you are on a fine, wide and grassy pathway which also marks the boundary of **Rutland**. You are walking on a ridge which is 600 ft high and gives excellent views.

5 Turn left to follow the bridleway until it appears to end in a cul-de-sac. Go left through an open metal gate at the 'end' of the bridleway into an arable field where you will find that the grass track continues round the field. Do not go through an inviting gap into the next field but stay where you are, following the hedgeline and keeping it on your left. Carry straight on through several fields for about ¾ mile passing through gaps in each field along a clear route. Eventually, a large patch of woodland comes into view ahead. This is **Prior's Coppice**. Turn left through an open wooden gate into a pasture field. Follow the track around the field to a narrow gap in the hedge on the far side. You now emerge on to a very wide grassy track between ash trees. In 200 yards this narrows, then widens a little, finally becoming a stone track and then **Wood Lane**.

6 This joins the **Brooke–Braunston road** and you turn left for a pleasant stroll downhill into **Braunston** passing farm buildings and bridges over the **Gwash** as you see the church ahead.

PLACE OF INTEREST NEARBY

Oakham, 2 miles distant, is the capital of England's smallest county. The castle with its massive collection of horseshoes, the Rutland County Museum, and the buttercross, are just a few of its attractions. Telephone: 01572 758441.

The Dog & Gun

T HIS WALK TAKES YOU THROUGH THE CLASSIC LANDSCAPE OF MEDIEVAL DESERTED VILLAGES IN THE BOULDER CLAY COUNTRY OF EASTERN LEICESTERSHIRE. ALTHOUGH THE LOST VILLAGES OF QUENBY, BAGGRAVE AND LOWESBY ARE CLOSE BY, IT IS THE FAMOUS SITE AT INGARSBY WHICH IS THE GEM AND WHICH CAN BE SEEN SO CLEARLY ON THE GROUND.

———————— ●◆● ————————

A prehistoric routeway crosses the area from Ingarsby to Covert Lane, Scraptoft, and a former railway line with many embankments and cuttings features along the walk. There is a strong sense of the past as you walk along and also a feeling of remoteness, and the beauty of the gently undulating terrain is a constant delight.

THE DOG & GUN is tucked away in one of Leicestershire's quietest villages. The cosy lounge and bar are very inviting and often full, as many people from Leicester's suburbs can dash out quickly for a snack and a drink. This Everards pub has Tiger, Beacon, Traditional Mild, Guinness and a guest beer. Strongbow cider is on draught. Drinking times: 12 noon to 2 pm every day (Sunday 4 pm) and 6 pm to 11 pm (Sunday 10.30 pm). There is a patio (in lieu of a garden) where children, adults and dogs can congregate.

Excellent and reasonably-priced bar food is available from 12 noon to 2 pm every day and in the evening between 6 pm and 9 pm. Monday evening is pie night and Tuesday is Italian night. Food is available 12 noon to 3 pm Sunday but not on Sunday night. There is a good wine list in support. Dominoes, cribbage and petanque are played.

Incidentally, there are 10 pubs in the county called Dog & Gun and one Dog & Hedgehog.

✆ 01162 595226

How to get there: Keyham is about 3 miles off the A47 at Houghton on the Hill. Follow the sign down a country lane via Ingarsby. Alternatively, you can reach Keyham from Leicester via Scraptoft.
Parking: There is a large car park at the Dog & Gun.
Length of the walk: 4 miles. Map: OS Landranger 141 or OS Explorer 233 (GR 669065).

THE WALK

① On leaving the **Dog & Gun** turn left into **Snow's Lane**. Bear left down the lane ignoring the footpath sign on your right. The bridleway you soon reach goes through private property, a boarding kennels and cattery, but do not be put off by barking dogs as you are entitled to use this path. Go forward to a wooden gate opposite and follow a grass track between hedges. Pass through a side gate to the left of a white wooden gate. Then turn left across a small stream and through a white gate going uphill diagonally to a stile and plank bridge in the far corner (arrow).

2 Cross to the path on the other side and follow to the left. At an open metal gate turn sharp right along a hedge (do not go straight on). At the corner of the field go through two gates over the old railway. **Billesdon Coplow** is in the distance. Carry on along to the left of the hedge to the gate ahead. Continue straight forward into the next field, also to the left of the hedge. Pass gates to your right and go on to the metal gate ahead in the corner of the field.

Cross the field to a gate at the left corner then go ahead to a gate at the far side. Go through a rickety metal gate and turn left onto a wide grass track. In 50 yards go through a wooden gate into rough pasture. Now go diagonally across the rough pasture, as an arrow indicates, to a telegraph pole and gate beyond. Pass through this gate and ahead are the mounds of the lost village of **Ingarsby**.

3 Go ahead to the motte known as **Monk's Grave** which is above the main village site. Pass round the mound and go downhill to a gap on a country lane. Turn left along this and go over the bridge, looking left at the old fish ponds and right to see the ridge and furrow of the old village. Leicester Abbey once owned the village but it was depopulated in 1469 when it was turned over to the more profitable sheep farming.

4 As you proceed along the lane you pass **Ingarsby Old Hall** on your left. This was probably the site of a monastic grange but some parts date from 1470. There are enlargements dating from 1579 and it was refronted in 1706. Go beyond the Hall entrance, ignoring the footpath sign here and carrying on a little further until you have passed under the old railway 'bridge'. Perhaps you can see to your right the former railway station, now nicely converted to a house? Look on your left for a

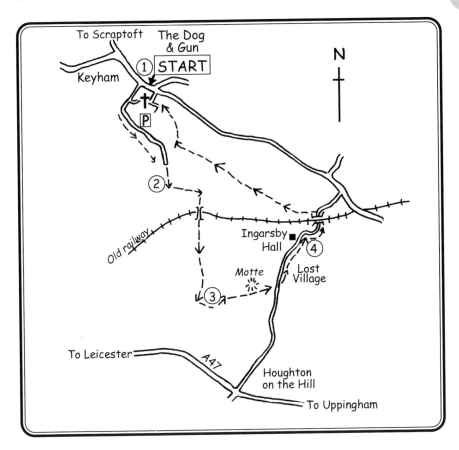

footpath sign (arrow) which may be overgrown. Here, cross the stile into a field and follow the hedge on your left across the field. At the corner keep close to the stream and cross a fence to a yellow post beyond the hedge. Carry on at the edge of the stream around the field (marker post indicates). Eventually you reach a yellow post around the far corner. Turn left to cross a stile near the stream (arrow) and keep to the left-hand side of the next field.

You reach a good track. Turn right to follow it uphill. In 50 yards cross a stile to the left (arrow). At the opposite side of a small paddock cross to a gate (arrow). Go over a stile and walk ahead to a white marker post. Climb a wooden fence and cross a field to an arrow on a fence post straight ahead. Go under a wire fence at an arrow post then ahead to another fence and arrow. This indicates diagonally across the field to the right of a pylon, crossing a couple of fences on the way. There is a yellow arrow to the right of the pylon.

Cross a stile and turn left diagonally towards the far corner of the field. In undergrowth there is a yellow marker post and stile. Cross, turning right along a narrow path behind some houses. Follow the path round to the left, also between buildings (arrow) with a fence on your right. The village lane is now on your left and so you can follow the **Main Street** back to the **Dog & Gun**.

There is a well-situated seat facing the church where you can pause and reflect on your walk. A red telephone box, village pump, and shining weathercock remind us of the typical English village. The charming church of All Saints is warmly brown in the sun. There are memorials to the Miles family and sad tablets to losses in the First World War. Keyham is potentially a good place to live, for it is reported that, in the past at least, 'there was an impressive longevity of the inhabitants, with people living to the great ages of 70, 80, 92 and beyond'.

PLACE OF INTEREST NEARBY

Why not visit the **National Space Centre** in Leicester, just 4 miles away. It is the UK's largest attraction dedicated to space and there are plenty of interactive displays. Telephone: 0870 607 7223.

The Queen's Head

THE WALK STARTS BEYOND THE CHURCH IN BILLESDON AND CROSSES KATE'S HILL IN THE DIRECTION OF SKEFFINGTON VALE FARM – ABOUT 1 MILE OF FIELD WALKING. IT CONTINUES VIA GATED ROADS THROUGH PARKLAND TO ROLLESTON AND BACK TO BILLESDON. THERE ARE MANY WIDE AND PLEASANT VIEWS ALL ROUND.

━━━━●●━━━━

Billesdon is a large, compact village with many old buildings, including the church and school nearby. There are lovely street scenes with quaint thatched cottages, very well kept. Once the A47 ran straight through the village but the bypass has brought quiet now. You can see where the busy road ran by the 'ragged' edge which will, in time, recover to match the historic centre. Look for the plaque on the school wall detailing its interesting history.

THE QUEEN'S HEAD is an Everards pub, situated in a lovely lane which curves gently towards the church. The pub lies at right angles to the lane so that the best view of the thatched 17th-century building is as you enter. Across the yard there are other buildings which are part of the pub. A conservatory/dining area has been added to the main building, but this does not mar the olde worlde appearance. Inside, low beams and wooden bench seats give a cosy and historic feel to the bar. Old Original, Tiger and Adnams ales are available, also keg cider. Drinking times are 11 am to 3 pm and 5 pm to 11 pm weekdays, Saturday all day and all day Sunday from 12 noon.

The pub has a restaurant and the full menu is available from 12 noon to 2 pm and 7 pm to 9.30 pm; Saturday 11.30 am to 2 pm and 7 pm to 9.30 pm; and Sunday carvery 12.30 pm to 2.30 pm only. A specials board lists bar food, game and fish being popular choices. There is a garden area for families. There is also a children's play area and petanque piste.

✆ 01162 596352

How to get there: Billesdon is just off the A47, about 8 miles east of Leicester. The Queen's Head is in Church Street.
Parking: There is a good car park at the pub, so you can avoid parking in the narrow village streets. If you intend to walk first, please try to contact someone at the pub to seek permission to leave your car.
Length of the walk: 4 miles. Map: OS Landranger series 141, or OS Explorer 233 (GR 720026).

THE WALK

1 Turn right from the **Queen's Head** into **Church Street**. Follow the road as it passes the school and carry on until you reach the road signs to **Tur Langton** and **Rolleston**. Ahead you will see a field gate about 100 yards further on to your left with a footpath sign.

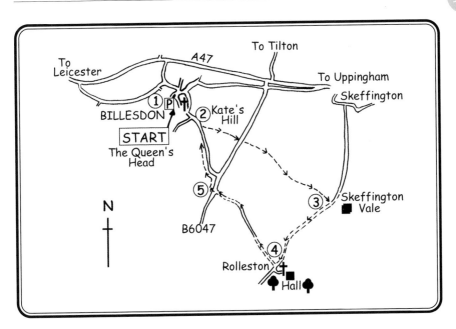

2 Go into the field, which is well marked by ridge and furrow. Cross the field diagonally uphill keeping a mound to your left. This is **Kate's Hill**. At the far side there is a gate about 100 yards from the left-hand corner of the field. Go through and into the next field. Although you may be able to walk directly across this field to the far side it will be better to follow the hedge round on your left. This brings you to a stile and plank bridge over a ditch and then onto the B6047 road to **Market Harborough**. Take care as you cross this road. You will find another stile opposite. When you have crossed this, keep to the high ground and aim for the left-hand corner of the hedge in front. Walk with the hedge on your right towards a wooden gate ahead.

Go through and then across to follow a hedge on your right. As it bears right you keep straight on to a clump of trees in a river valley. At the far right side of the field you will find a bridle gate. Go through and then turn sharp right to a cement bridge over a stream about 30 yards away. Climb up a slope and over a broken fence into the next field. Continue uphill to the hedge on your right and follow this until just before you reach a kink in the hedge. Here there is a gap. Turn right through it and, at once, left over a fence into the next field. Cross, bearing right, to a gap in the hedge at the far side. Here, climb a fence (wire and wood) into the next field then turn left to a metal gate with a footpath sign which is also opposite the drive to **Skeffington Vale Farm**.

3 You have now reached the gated road to **Rolleston**. Turn right for a most pleasant walk through lovely parkland. The road has a stream and woodland to your right and you will cross two bridges. Shortly, you climb uphill to **Rolleston**. As you go through a metal gate into the village area you will see a signpost showing 'Gated Road to Billesdon 1½ miles' which you must eventually follow to return to your starting point.

Before you do return, go to look at the 'village'. If you go down the **Tugby bridleway** it will lead you to the church and Tudor manor house close by. This is a lovely setting and there are walled gardens nearby.

4 When you are ready, go back to the gated road to **Billesdon**. The gated road is clear as it undulates in front of you. In 1 mile you reach the B6047.

5 Turn right for 200 yards. Walk on the verge and beware of traffic here. When you reach the lane leading down into **Billesdon** turn left and follow this for ¾ mile into the village.

PLACE OF INTEREST NEARBY

Wistow Rural Centre and maize maze is approximately 5 miles west, near the A6. The rural centre is a very large garden centre with a shop and café, and, in season, the maze provides hours of fun for all the family. Telephone: 07884 403 889.

The Bewicke Arms

THE WALK FOLLOWS GOADBY LANE FOR 2 MILES THEN TURNS SOUTH TOWARDS CRANOE. IT SUBSEQUENTLY GOES NORTH-EASTWARDS PAST THE LOST VILLAGE OF OTHORPE AND IN 1¾ MILES REACHES HALLATON. THERE ARE EXCELLENT VIEWS ALL ROUND FOR MUCH OF THE WALK, WHICH IS LARGELY THROUGH ENORMOUS ARABLE FIELDS, SURELY ONE OF THE BEST EXAMPLES IN BRITAIN OF 'PRAIRIE FARMING'.

●◆●

This is a beautiful part of east Leicestershire with plentiful streams, tiny valleys and well-dissected landscape. It is the area of heavy clay so boots are advisable. Do the walk on a fine day, if you can, and you will see the locality at its best. Hallaton, in itself, could occupy half a day at least, with its duck pond, village green, butter cross, war memorial, motte and bailey castle site (one of the finest in the country), and St Michael's church. There is an excellent small museum in Hog Lane, where you can find out about the pagan ceremony which takes place each year on Easter Monday in Hare Pie Bank, known as the Hallaton Bottle-Kicking Event. After a huge hare pie has been cut and distributed, teams from Hallaton and Medbourne (as well as anyone else who wants to take part) fight to gain possession of two wooden casks filled with ale.

THE BEWICKE ARMS, a 400-year-old thatched country inn, faces the village green with its old butter cross, in probably the best of Leicestershire villages. A warm and friendly atmosphere is backed up by efficient service and excellent food and drink. The inside may not be quite so breath-taking as the outside but the two oddly-shaped rooms – the Bottle Kicking Bar and Snug – have a real atmosphere, with their old fashioned settles, some with high backs and wings, plus the decor of deer heads and farming implements.

The bar food is largely home-made with delicious soup, daily fish specials, for example New Zealand mussels in a tasty sauce, smoked haddock and mushroom pancake, and swordfish steaks, followed by excellent lemon cheesecake. Daily specials change with the season. There is a children's menu and meal times are 12 noon to 2 pm and 7 pm to 9.30 pm every day. The award-winning tearoom is open from 10 am to 5 pm (4 pm in winter).

Very well-kept real ales include Flowers IPA and guest ales on handpump, served between 12 noon to 2.30 pm and 7 pm to 11 pm, Sundays 12 noon to 2.30 pm.

How to get there: Hallaton is a large village 17 miles east of Leicester, and just 2½ miles south of the A47 at East Norton. An alternative route is from Uppingham on the B664 via Horninghold.
Parking: The Bewicke Arms has a large car park but there is also ample street parking in the village.
Length of the walk: 5½ miles. Map: OS Landranger series 141, or OS Explorer 233 (GR 787966).

Children can join you anywhere and there is a garden area (where dogs are welcome to wait) overlooking a pleasant valley. Picnic tables are located on this terrace. This freehouse also has en suite accommodation.

✆ 01858 555217

THE WALK

1 On leaving the **Bewicke Arms,** turn left to the church. As you approach note the fine 14th-century broach spire and octagonal pinnacle. Bear right into **Churchgate** past a row of lovely old cottages and turn the corner with the school on your left.

2 Bear right and do not take the footpath which you see well signed at the next bend. Instead, carry on up **Goadby Lane,** taking in the excellent view of the motte and bailey site on your left. Note also prolific ridge and furrow around. Soon you cross a deeply-incised valley at a ford. Should the stream be full take the route via the plank bridge. All around is heavy clay land, mostly enormous arable fields. The route is very undulating. As you climb up a gentle ridge you eventually cross a large arable field and at the far side, to your left, you then see a yellow marker post with a blue arrow pointing into the field on your left.

3 Turn in that direction and follow the hedge line until you reach the far right corner of this huge field where you will find a gate marked with a blue arrow. This indicates that you must go straight ahead following the hedge on your left. When this hedge turns left you must keep straight on. Do not be tempted by gates and signs on your left.

Straight in front you will find a wooden gate marked by a yellow post. Go through this gate and, again, straight ahead following the tree line and passing a small pond on your left. When you arrive at the corner of the field go through the metal gate ahead (arrow). Follow the hedge line downhill. Soon you

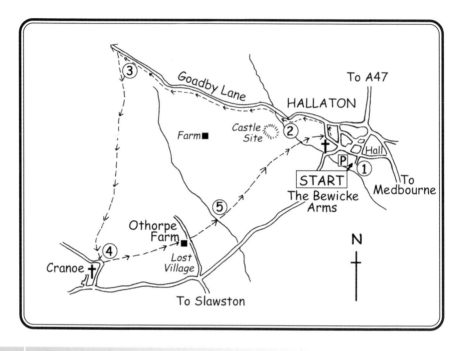

reach a footpath sign on your right. Here you will eventually need to turn left to cross the field to find a stile and marker post at the far side.

Before doing so, however, you should carry on into **Cranoe** to see **St Michael's church** opposite the **Old Rectory**. The base of the tower is 13th-century and there is a Norman font, but storm damage in 1846 led to rebuilding in 1846-49. This village was once owned by the Brudenell family of Deene Park, Northants, better known for the Earl of Cardigan (1797-1868), the 7th Earl who led the Charge of the Light Brigade at Balaclava in 1854.

4 After this diversion, you have returned to the stile previously mentioned (well-signposted). Bear right alongside the hedge to **Othorpe Farm** which you can see ahead. At the corner of the arable field a marker post points ahead so that you follow alongside the hedge to your left, until you reach a gate at the far side into a farm paddock and a handgate in the corner. In the farmyard an arrow indicates that you must turn left until you reach a metal gate. Ahead, marker posts show your route directly across the field to double gates and a plank bridge over a stream.

5 Go next to marker posts on the hill slope ahead. Here you can see the next marker post at a gap in the hedge on the far side. When you get to this point you realise that it is an open wooden handgate. Go through into a very big field but instead of taking the indicated route go diagonally across the field to the left. At the far left-hand side you will see a double stile. Cross it and go on to the next yellow marker post bearing right. At the marker post follow the arrow, bearing right, and in the distance note another post at the corner of the cemetery. At the far side of the field find a wooden stile, but before you do you must cross the stream via a plank bridge.

This is a marvellous valley for geographers – it has terracettes, cut-off meanders, ox-bow lakes, river cliffs, slip-off slopes and, to complete the scene, up-valley, in a strategic position, the motte and bailey site is located. Who could ask for anything more?

Carry on to the marker post at the corner of the cemetery and follow round the edge to reach a metal gate leading onto the village lane. Turn right to return to the centre of the village and the **Bewicke Arms**.

PLACE OF INTEREST NEARBY

A few miles to the south is the ancient village of **Medbourne**, originally a Roman settlement. With its large elegant houses, stones cottages and medieval bridge crossing a tributary of the river Welland, it is well worth exploring.

The Black Horse

FOXTON IS AN ATTRACTIVE VILLAGE SITUATED NEAR THE MARKET HARBOROUGH 'ARM' OF THE GRAND UNION CANAL. THIS ROUTE INCLUDES A STROLL AROUND FOXTON BEFORE FOLLOWING THE TOWPATH TO FOXTON LOCKS AND THEN RETURNING FROM BOTTOM LOCK VIA A COUNTRY LANE.

Most people come to Foxton to see the locks which are about half a mile from the village. Ascending these famous locks, which are one of the outstanding sights in Britain, the full panorama of the staircase of ten locks can be seen. However, there is lots more to see at Foxton, including St Andrew's church standing on a hill above the village, opposite the Black Horse pub, Monk Hall, the Old Court House and the Baptist chapel.

FOXTON – *The Black Horse*

THE BLACK HORSE was rebuilt in 1900 and is just outside the village. One attraction of the Black Horse is that it looks just like a large house and this is especially so when viewed from the large garden at the rear. Children are welcome.

A conservatory restaurant provides excellent facilities and the home-cooked food ranges from snacks to complete meals with enough choice for all tastes. Vegetarian meals are included. Booking is advisable, particularly on Sundays when food is served from 12 noon to 4 pm. Food is available the rest of the week from 12 noon to 3 pm and 6 pm to 9 pm. Drinking times are 11 am to 3 pm and 5 pm to 11 pm weekdays, 12 noon to 10.30 pm Sundays.

There is a traditional yet informal atmosphere in the pub, which serves Greene King beers as well as traditional draught ales. In a separate building across the driveway there is a games area which includes a skittle alley, providing a focus for local entertainment. Jazz and country and western evenings are held on a weekly basis. Accommodation is also available.

✆ 01858 545250

> **How to get there:** Foxton is 4 miles north-west of Market Harborough and is close to the A6. You can also approach the village via the A427, then follow signs from Lubenham.
> **Parking:** There is a good car park to the rear of the Black Horse.
> **Length of the walk:** 2 miles. Map: OS Landranger series 141 or OS Explorer 233 and 223 (GR 700900).

THE WALK

1 On leaving the **Black Horse** turn left downhill into **Main Street**. Go over the canal bridge and turn sharp left into **North Lane** and then onto the canal towpath to your left. Now turn left again to follow the canal towpath under the bridge you just crossed. As you walk along, you pass the old school, now a field

PUB WALKS IN LEICESTERSHIRE & RUTLAND

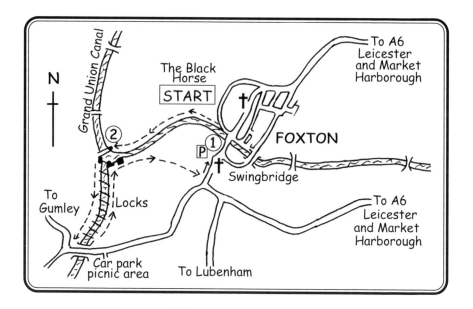

centre, originally built in 1876. You come to the **swingbridge** which must be turned to allow barges to pass.

Turn left into **Swingbridge Road** and look for a footpath on your left which will take you into **Middle Street**, near to **Monk Hall**. Robert Monk left the village over 70 years ago and was so successful in the hotel business in Leicester that when he died he was able to leave a large sum of money to build the Hall and set up a trust fund.

Turn right to go down to the end of **Middle Street**. Did you see the old mud wall on the left, often used by bees when laying their eggs in burrows which they make in the wall? At the end of the street turn left round into **Main Street**. Look for the small village green and the **Old Court House**. Further down on your right is the **Baptist chapel** which is built of local bricks and was founded in 1716. **Foxton** had a strong Nonconformist element in its population at that time.

Still going down **Main Street** look for the **Shoulder of Mutton**, set back from the road in quite an imposing position. Formerly this was a farmhouse, licensed when greater business was expected due to the building of the Barge Lift. At this time, too, the **Black Horse** was rebuilt (1900).

When you reach the canal bridge again, turn right into **North Lane** and once more left to join the canal towpath, but this time turn right to follow it to **Foxton Locks**.

2 You reach the main canal basin in just over ½ mile. This is a lovely scene to ponder on for a while. Then bear right along the towpath to cross bridge 62. Go under bridge 61 at **Bottom Lock** then carry on at the side of the ten locks until you reach the top, returning down the other side back to the shop and the pub at bridge 61, a freehouse with real ale as well as a fine patio where you can watch the canal activity.

Thomas Telford advised on the construction of **Foxton Locks** which were built between 1808 and 1814. The **Market Harborough arm** was opened in 1809. When the link into Northamptonshire was finally made to the **Grand Junction Canal** at **Long Buckby**, a daily service could be offered to all parts of England. Since the passage through the locks took at least one hour a quicker alternative was devised in 1900, namely an inclined plane at the side. However, due to a reduction in traffic it was dismantled in 1911, even though it had reduced the transit time to 8 minutes.

As you come out of **Foxton Locks Inn**, turn left, cross the bridge and join the bridle path to the right of **Foxton Boat Services**. Follow a rough road to the main road ½ mile away. Here there is a cemetery to your right at the corner. Turn left downhill to reach **St Andrew's church** on its ancient hill site and then return to the start.

PLACE OF INTEREST NEARBY

Nearby is **Market Harborough**, with its old grammar school, museum, plenty of excellent small shops and a very pleasant canalside walk.

The Cross Keys

OUR WALK STARTS IN BURBAGE AND PASSES THROUGH ESTATES BEFORE REACHING THE A5070 IN ½ MILE. THENCE IT PENETRATES BURBAGE WOOD AND GOES UNDER THE RAILWAY LINE, MAKING FOR THE VISITOR CENTRE AT THE FAR SIDE OF THE COMMON. THE RETURN IS VIA A DIFFERENT PATH THROUGH THE WOODS. ALL ROUTES ARE MOST PLEASANT, EASY, LEVEL AND CONTRASTING AS WELL AS BEING WELL WAYMARKED.

●◆●

According to W.G. Hoskins 'Burbage is a most interesting place to explore: it was once a flourishing little country town, now overshadowed by Hinckley two miles away, and it contains a good deal of praiseworthy building from the late-16th to the mid-19th century, especially in and around the broad street by the church'. As part of the town's interesting past, the landscape just to the north has two valuable features: Burbage Wood and Burbage

BURBAGE – *The Cross Keys*

Common, both as significant and important as the fine old buildings in the town. They are 200 acres (80 ha) in area, including woodland, scrub and grassland with a rich variety of flora and fauna. There are two natural woodlands - Burbage Wood and Sheepy Wood containing oak, ash, maple with hazel below, probably the remnants of the medieval Hinckley Forest. They are still managed by coppicing which you can usually see on your walk. The common was owned by the manorial estate and commoners could graze livestock on it by right. It is rich in plants and animals. In damper places marsh forget-me-not and ragged robin thrive, whilst in better drained soils there is spiny restharrow, lesser stitchwort and tormentil. It is favoured by butterflies such as the orange-tip and comma. Kestrels hover above and whitethroats and meadow pipits breed there.

THE CROSS KEYS is a Marston's pub, on the main street which is quite busy but has a pleasant outlook to the church with several older houses around. It is unpretentious outside and inside there is a good atmosphere and the feel of a genuine local, with a darkish lounge, a snug with pew-like seats, and an open fire.

Marston's traditional ales are available, with Strongbow cider. Drinking times are 12 noon to 11 pm Monday to Saturday and Sunday 12 noon to 10.30 pm. There is no pretence to haute cuisine but hunger will be well satisfied by home-cooked food every day 12 noon to 4 pm and 6.30 pm to 9.30 pm.

How to get there: Burbage is in south-west Leicestershire only 2 miles away from Watling Street (the A5) and the M69 is even closer via the A5070. Hinckley and Burbage are situated very near to each other in the triangle made by the A5 and the M69, the Leicester–Birmingham railway line dividing the two places.
Parking: No pub car park, but there is good street parking close to the church and in nearby streets.
Length of the walk: 4½ miles. Map: OS Landranger 140 or OS Explorer 233 (GR 442928).

PUB WALKS IN LEICESTERSHIRE & RUTLAND

There is a long garden with a separate children's room and a cricket pitch at the end. Well-behaved dogs are welcome in the garden and in the pub at evening time.

✆ 01455 239443

THE WALK

1 Turn left on leaving the **Cross Keys** and walk on for about 300 yards until you reach **Woodland Avenue** on your right. Go down this road to **Meadow Drive,** turning left and then right. Bear right again into **Winchester Road** and now carry on to the A5070. Cross this road carefully to a sign opposite, 'Burbage Woods & Common'.

2 Go through a gap between the buildings to a metal gate. Climb the stile at the side into the pasture field. Walk along the hedge and in about 150 yards you will see a stile on your left. Cross this into the field, turning sharp right to follow the hedge. At the corner of this field you turn right across a stile into **Burbage Wood.** Turn left and keep to the edge of the wood. Ignore pathways, however important they may look, to your right. Soon you reach the end of the wood and go through a wooden handgate, across a plank bridge into a rough meadow. Go straight ahead to the railway bridge you will see. To your left is **Woodhouse Farm** which sometimes provides refreshments.

3 Go under the railway bridge and keep between two blue marker posts ahead. You are now on the common and if you go straight ahead you will arrive at the **Visitor Centre** in ½ mile. This houses a display (free of charge) interpreting the site, as well as a souvenir shop. Guided walks and talks are available from time to time.

4 When you are ready you can return by the same route to the railway bridge. If you prefer, however, there are several different paths which will bring you to the same point, for example, one

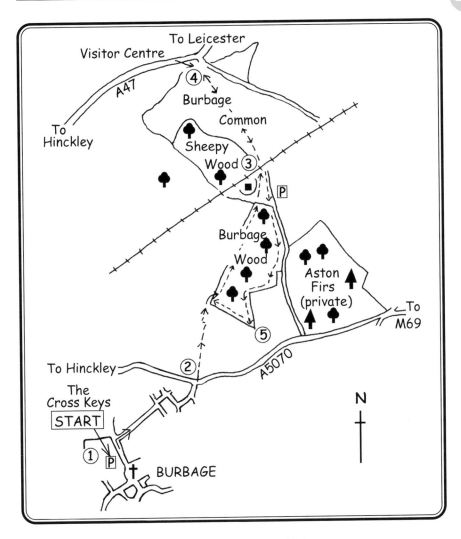

is through **Sheepy Wood**. Information boards will give further details.

As you return under the railway bridge go towards the left-hand corner of the pasture field. Follow the stream along, which is on your left. You then see blue marker posts indicating a lane – **Smithy Lane**. Close by there are picnic tables. Cross a plank bridge into a small car park. At the far left side there is a small handgate. Turn right through it, over a wooden bridge into the wood. Turn left along a woodland path and at a path crossroads keep straight on.

5 At a T-junction turn right. Follow this path, but then bear left keeping on the edge of the wood. When the path bears right you will see the spire of **Burbage church** to your left.

Carry on to a stile at the corner of the wood in front of you, keeping to the left of a litter bin. This is the same stile by which you entered the wood earlier on. Cross it and turn left to follow along the hedgeside. When you reach the stile on your left which leads into the pasture field where you first started, cross it and make your way back to the A5070. Return via **Winchester Road, Meadow Drive** and **Woodland Avenue** to the centre of **Burbage**.

PLACE OF INTEREST NEARBY

In Lower Bond Street, Hinckley, can be found the **Hinckley & District Museum** housed in restored 17th-century framework knitters' cottages. The museum contains displays on the hosiery industry and the history of the town, as well as on the Battle of Bosworth. Telephone: 01455 251218.

The Cock Inn

THIS WALK IS IN THE PLEASANTLY UNDULATING CLAYLANDS OF WEST LEICESTERSHIRE, IN THE VICINITY OF THE ROMAN WATLING STREET AND QUITE CLOSE TO THE RIVER SENCE WHICH JOINS THE RIVER ANKER NEAR KING DICK'S HOLE, JUST BEYOND RATCLIFFE CULEY. THE ROUTE IS RECTANGULAR, CROSSING THE FIELDS FROM SIBSON TO SHEEPY PARVA, THEN OVER THE SENCE AT THE OLD MILL TO SHEEPY MAGNA, GOING SOUTH TO RATCLIFFE CULEY AND FOLLOWING THE COUNTRY LANE EAST UNTIL AGAIN CROSSING THE FIELDS ON A RURAL SHORT CUT WITH SIBSON IN SIGHT ON A HILL. BE PREPARED FOR SOME MUD AS YOU PASS NEAR STREAMS.

All three villages (four with Sheepy Parva) have points of interest and some good buildings. The churches are certainly worth looking into. For example, at Ratcliffe Culey the early 14th-century church has a moated homestead site to the south-east, whilst at Sheepy Magna there is a fine medieval tithe barn at Newhouse Grange, ½ mile to the north-west. Ratcliffe Culey means the red cliff or bank held by Hugo de Culy in 1285 and Sheepy may mean a dry island where sheep might safely graze. Just a few miles south of this walk is the Roman settlement of Mancetter – at least the site of it. You can see that though this may seem a neglected area to some, it has many secrets for you to discover on the walk.

Situated on a corner, the **COCK INN** is both attractive and interesting outside and inside. This is an old building dating from 1250 and it was owned by the church until 1939. Its first full licence was granted in 1954. The thatch, black/white timbering, lattice windows and low doorways all reveal its age as does the wattle and daub wall inside and the lovely small, low-beamed rooms. There are snug places for everyone it seems, all tucked away very nicely. All around one is aware of antiquity. There are seats outside at the back to make use of on fine days, as well as tables on a patio.

    The popular Stable Restaurant has both à la carte and table d'hôte menus and specialises in all kinds of mouth-watering dishes which are home-made. The bar menu includes steak and kidney pie, honey roast ham, Scottish steaks grilled to taste, and there are also children's dishes. These are all available 11.30 am to 2 pm and 6.30 pm to 9.45 pm weekdays, Sundays 12 noon to 2 pm and 7 pm to 9.30 pm (restaurant closed on Sunday night). Children are welcome in the eating area and restaurant. This is a Punch Taverns house with well-kept Bass, Hook Norton, a variety of lagers and

How to get there: Sibson is in the far west of the county about 18 miles away from Leicester. In fact, it is nearer to Tamworth. Market Bosworth is about 4 miles to the north-east. From the West Midlands the best approach is via the M42 joining the A5 at junction 10 and then turning onto the A444. From Coventry and Nuneaton it is easy to travel along the A444. From Leicester one suitable and scenic route is via Desford and Market Bosworth to the A444.
Parking: Excellent parking at the Cock Inn.
Length of the walk: 5½ miles. Map: OS Landranger series 140 or OS Explorer 232 (GR 355009).

Strongbow and Woodpecker cider. Drinking times are 11.30 am to 2.30 pm and 6.30 pm to 11 pm weekdays, Sundays 12 noon to 3 pm and 7 pm to l0.30 pm.

You would be wise to do the walk first as once you are established inside this lovely old pub you may not want to leave in a hurry.

☎ 01827 880357

THE WALK

1 Leave the Cock Inn via the front door and turn left into the village lane. If you are parked in the pub car park go out into the village lane also turning left. Proceed down the lane until you reach the right-angled bend. Look for **Glenfield Cottage** and **Vine Cottage** on your left. The pathway is between the two and you must enter a handgate to **Glenfield Cottage,** then follow the path behind the houses, bearing left until you reach a stile.

2 Keep the hedge on your right and go over another stile. Go straight ahead across a field to a telegraph pole following the line of a fence. At a yellow mark on one of the poles go through a gate and follow a hedge line. Cross a plank bridge at a yellow marker turning into a gate on your right. Then follow the hedge on your left to a yellow marker post near a barn. Cross a stile into a ploughed field and go across to the far side to the left of some trees. With the trees on your right go to a marker post ahead. At the next post go diagonally right to a telegraph post and the next yellow marker. Turn left to cross a stile. Keep to the hedge on your left following the line of telegraph poles. Cross a plank bridge and go ahead to the next stile and plank bridge.

3 Now **Sheepy Parva** comes into view ahead and the way is clear across three stiles, each with an arrow. The telegraph poles veer off to the left away from you. Go ahead to a metal gate which leads onto a country lane. Turn left and follow it round passing **Moat House** on your left. Turn left into **Mill Lane** (B585). Carry

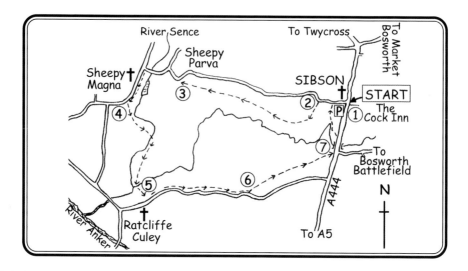

on and you will turn into Sheepy Magna. After crossing a large Mill Pond you turn sharp left into the village street where you will find a post office, a shop, the **Black Horse** and the church.

④ In ¼ mile, as you begin to leave the village centre, look for a sign on the left side of the lane 'Footpath to Ratcliffe Culey'. Go over the stile (arrow) here and cross to a yellow marker post ahead. Follow the stream round a little but then turn in a 2 o'clock direction to another post on the far side of the field. Cross the bridge here and turn right to follow the stream. At the river bend climb a double stile and plank bridge (arrow). Cross the field to the far right corner (marker post). **Ratcliffe Culey** is ahead on a ridge. Cross a stile and follow the hedge on your right to a wooden bridge at the far side. Then go ahead uphill towards the church spire. You arrive at a farmyard behind some village houses. Go over a fence into a green track between the houses and you come to the village street with a red telephone box opposite you.

⑤ Turn left to walk along the lane leading from **Ratcliffe** to the A444 for 1 mile. Just beyond **Barn Farm**, on your right, look for a footpath pole. This is the route across the fields to **Sibson** which you can see on a ridge in the distance. Its church is distinctive.

6) Cross the stile here and follow the hedge on your left to a yellow marker post in the corner. Cross this stile and then go diagonally right across a large field to a post in the far hedge. Go through a gap then through a gate opposite across to a yellow post at the rear of a farmhouse. Cross a stile and plank bridge going ahead to the next stile. Turn left and follow the hedge on your right to the next post and stile behind the farm. Cross and go to the left of a pond towards the next post and stile ahead. Cross to the stile and plank bridge opposite, keeping the hedge on your left. You arrive at the gate to a bungalow. This is the right of way and you are permitted to go through it then onto a farm drive bearing right to the main road (A444).

7) Turn left and keep to the verge. Cross the bridge where you see the sign to **Sibson**. After about 100 yards you come to a footpath sign on your left just before reaching **Miller's Hotel**. Cross the stile here (arrow) and bear right diagonally to the far corner. The stream is on your left. Cross a stile and follow the new fencing to the village ahead – the church is in front of you and soon you arrive at a metal gate. Follow the road between an estate of palatial houses and at the village lane turn right to arrive back at the **Cock Inn**.

PLACE OF INTEREST NEARBY

Bosworth Battlefield Visitor Centre and Country Park is about 3 miles to the east. It includes a film theatre, book and gift shop, trails, picnic area, restaurant and children's playground. The car parks and footpaths are open all year during daylight hours. Telephone: 01455 290429.

The Battlefield Line Railway runs from the site to Shackerstone, 5 miles away. Telephone: 01827 880754.

Nemo's Bar and Diner

THIS IS A WALK INTO LEICESTERSHIRE'S INDUSTRIAL PAST. STARTING AT STONEY COVE, ONCE A THRIVING QUARRY AREA KNOWN AS LANE'S HILL, INCLUDING TOP QUARRY AND STANTON TOP PIT, THE WALK CROSSES THE RIVER SOAR AS IT MAKES A SHARP RIGHT-ANGLED BEND ON ITS WAY TO FLOW THROUGH CENTRAL LEICESTER. CLOSE BY, ½ MILE TO THE EAST, IS THE OLD ROMAN ROAD KNOWN AS THE FOSSE WAY, LATER THE A46. NO DOUBT THE ROMANS WERE THE FIRST TO QUARRY THE ROADSTONE NEARBY. IN THE DISTANCE CROFT HILL CAN BE SEEN, A REGIONAL FOCUS. NOTE THE CHARMING STREAM AND CHURCH AS YOU REACH CROFT, YOU THEN CROSS THE FIELDS FOR 1½ MILES UNTIL YOU ARRIVE AT STONEY STANTON WHERE YOU GO THROUGH THE VILLAGE TO RETURN TO STONEY COVE.

17

NEMO'S BAR AND DINER at Stoney Cove is one of the most interesting and invigorating eating houses within the county. It nestles below the 100-ft rocks of the quarry by a bay of clear spring water. The quarry is 35 metres deep and is the setting for the national Inland Dive Centre and Watersports. This was once a working granite quarry with valuable igneous rocks which also occur at other locations in the area such as Enderby, Narborough and Croft.

Inside Nemo's Bar, a large comfortable lounge has several cosy corners and there is a very long bar which usually means you are served quickly. There are lanterns, charts, ships' emblems and other nautical artefacts and in the ceiling a ship's wheel. The paved balconies allow good views of events on the lake. Children are welcome but must be supervised at all times.

The real ales are Tetley Bitter and draught Burton Ale with Calders available. Scrumpy Jack and Strongbow are on draught, as is Guinness. There is a very good range of lagers and non-alcoholic drinks. Drinking times are 11 am to 11 pm Monday to Saturday and 12 noon to 10.30 pm on Sundays during British Summer Time. When the clocks are changed to GMT they serve 11 am to 2.30 pm and 6.30 pm to 11 pm weekdays and all day Saturday and Sunday. Food times are 11.30 am to 2 pm and 6.30 pm to 9.30 pm weekdays and 11.30 am to 9.30 pm Saturday and Sunday.

✆ 01455 274198

How to get there: Stoney Cove is near to Stoney Stanton. Follow the sign to Sapcote from Stoney Stanton. Both villages are about 10 miles south-west of Leicester, quite close to the M69. You can approach from Hinckley via the A5070 and the B4069. The A5 is also close and you can take the B4114 to Sharnford and Sapcote if you approach from this direction. From Leicester take the A46 and B4114.

Parking: There are large car parking areas but Stoney Cove is busy seven days a week with divers, and waterside car parks may be full. There are outside car parks on the approach road.

Length of the walk: 5½ miles. Map: OS Landranger series 140 or OS Explorer 233 (GR 496941).

THE WALK

1 Walk out of **Stoney Cove** along the lane by which you first entered. At the main road turn right into the bridlepath signposted. As you follow this path you have good views of the Cove to your right. Go through a metal gate at the farm and then bear right along a cinder track to a telegraph pole where the track ends. Now turn left at the edge of the field and carry on to a handgate in the opposite corner of the next field. Go through and onto a cinder path which leads to the main road (arrow). To your left is the village of **Stoney Stanton**. Cross the road carefully to the bridlepath sign opposite. Walk straight ahead then bear slightly right to a gate at the far corner of the next field. Go through this metal gate, keeping the hedge on your left, making for a gap in the hedge at the corner of the field with a bridge beyond.

2 Cross the footbridge via a handgate (arrow) and over the arched stone bridge. This is the **river Soar**. Follow the hedgeline as it curves ahead of you on a wide grass track. **Croft Hill** can be seen in front. The track leads clearly into **Croft** village, via several

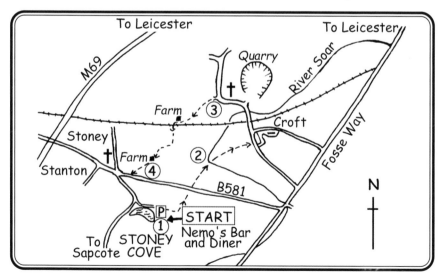

gates. As it comes to a lane you walk down this to the main road and turn left, then over a railway bridge with views to the huge complex of ECC Quarries on your right. Beware of lorry traffic on this stretch on working days. Cross the pretty stream then turn left uphill with the **Heathcote Arms** opposite. As you walk up **Huncote Road** keep to the upper pathway. Follow the road round past the church on the right. Go round the bend but turn left at the footpath sign just beyond the house.

3 Keep to the right of the cemetery gate, cross the stile and go diagonally to the far left corner. Cross a fence and concrete bridge over a small stream then follow a raised track towards a farmhouse. Go through the metal gate to the left of the farmhouse then turn left under the railway. Go straight ahead with the hedge on your right for about 250 yards. Look for the gap/fence in the hedge here. Turn right to cross this under the pylons. You need to aim for the far left corner of this field with **Stoney Stanton** church spire as a landmark ahead. You may find it easier to walk round the field boundary rather than across.

When you reach the corner cross a deep ditch and fence. Go diagonally to a gate at the far corner. Turn right through this gate into a muddy farm track. The right of way is over a stile on the left and then follows parallel to the farm drive. It then joins the drive as it leads into a village lane and then the main road, where you turn right.

4 Keep to the footpath, turning left at the crossroads signposted to Sapcote. Go down this road until, in a short distance, you reach the entry to Stoney Cove. Follow this lane back to the start.

PLACE OF INTEREST NEARBY

At nearby Kirkby Mallory, a few miles to the west, is Mallory Park, where its motor racing circuit is billed as 'the country's best spectator viewing circuit'. Telephone: 01455 842931.

The Bradgate

Tᴏ THE WALK STARTS AT THE BRADGATE AND YOU SHOULD TAKE TIME TO EXPLORE NEWTOWN LINFORD, FOR THIS LINEAR VILLAGE CONTAINS A VARIETY OF VERNACULAR HOUSES AND FARMS WHICH DEMONSTRATE THE USES OF LOCAL BUILDING MATERIALS EXCELLENTLY. THERE ARE ALSO MANY INSTANCES OF TIMBER-FRAMED BUILDINGS WITH PLASTER AND BRICK INFILLING. INDEED, BRADGATE HOUSE WAS ONE OF THE FIRST BUILDINGS IN BRITAIN TO USE BRICK, ALONG WITH NEARBY KIRBY MUXLOE CASTLE. THE CURVE OF THE STREET AND ATTRACTIVENESS OF BUILDINGS MAKES THIS A MEMORABLE VILLAGE SCENE. SOON THE WALK ENTERS BRADGATE PARK AND FOLLOWS THE RIVER LIN PASSING THE RUINS OF BRADGATE HOUSE, MOVING ALONGSIDE CROPSTON RESERVOIR, THEN ROUND COPPICE PLANTATION, ACROSS TO OLD JOHN VIA

SLIDING STONE WOOD AND BACK TO THE ENTRANCE DOWNHILL
PASSING TYBURN. YOU SHOULD LOOK INSIDE MARION'S COTTAGE
AS YOU GO OUT WHERE THERE ARE DISPLAYS ABOUT THE PARK AND
MANY PUBLICATIONS.

The spectacular scenery of Charnwood Forest is a sharp contrast to
the flat plains and valleys of the Midlands. It has been likened to a
'Little Switzerland' or a miniature Wales. Rocky crags formed out
of some of Britain's oldest strata punctuate the skyline, and
eminences such as Bardon Hill, Old John and Beacon Hill are very
well-known to local people. One of the outstanding parts of
Charnwood is Bradgate Park, near Newtown Linford. The river Lin
traverses the park and passes the ruins of Bradgate House, once the
home of Lady Jane Grey, the nine days' Queen of England. Deer
roam the park, and horses, cattle, sheep and rabbits have grazed
the area. There is much bracken – perhaps too much – and this has
to be controlled by burning and bruising. Heather has been re-
introduced in the hope that it may flourish again. There are spinneys
and plantations, many pines, but it is the pollarded oaks which
catch the eye. The story remains that they were beheaded in memory
of Lady Jane Grey.

How to get there: Newtown Linford is about 6 miles north-
west of Leicester and can be reached via the B5327 Anstey road
which is accessed from the A46 Leicester by-pass. Alternatively
leave the M1 at Junction 22 and follow signs to Bradgate Park
from the A511.
Parking: Although there is ample parking at the rear of the pub,
it is shared on occasions with the village hall across the road.
At these times, the car park can become rather congested and
it would probably be a good idea to phone the Bradgate prior
to your walk.
Length of the walk: 3½ miles. Map: OS Landranger series 129,
or OS Explorer 233 and 246 (GR 519100).

Pub Walks in Leicestershire & Rutland

THE BRADGATE INN is situated along the main street of Newtown Linford, within just 200 yards of the entrance to Leicestershire's premier beauty spot, Bradgate Park. The pub's exterior is typical of the village and the Charnwood area, with its sturdy granite construction, and presents a fine frontage to the street. To the rear are a large beer garden and a children's play area. The Mulberry Pub Company has run the pub since 2005 and has gained an enviable reputation for the quality of its service.

There is a good selection of food on offer from bar snacks such as soup and ploughman's through to tempting main meals such as steak and ale pie or the more exotic grilled swordfish. A full range of dishes can be viewed on the pub's website: www.mulberrypubco.com. Food is available from 12 noon to 2.30 pm and from 6 pm to 9 pm (to 9.30 pm on Friday and Saturday and from 12 noon to 6 pm on Sunday). The Bradgate is open all day during the summer.

Everard's real ales are on tap, as well as a comprehensive range of lagers, smooth ales and ciders. Wine is available either by the bottle or the glass.

✆ 01530 242239

THE WALK

1 On leaving the Bradgate turn left down the main street. You pass the church on your left. If time allows, go inside to see the odd ABCD tombstone which is about 15 ins by 3 ft. It has no name, only the letters of the alphabet in both capitals and small letters with two incomplete sets of Arabic numerals. Once it stood in the churchyard but was moved inside and attached to the wall behind the font. The origin is still a mystery.

Turn left into the car park leading into **Bradgate Park** and cross through the kissing gate to the road beyond. Follow the river as it passes through its 'gorge' section known as **Little Matlock**. Here the massive intrusive igneous rock contrasts with siltstones which you can see if you go over the bridge opposite the house ruins, into Stable Pit. Note the red clay river cliff from

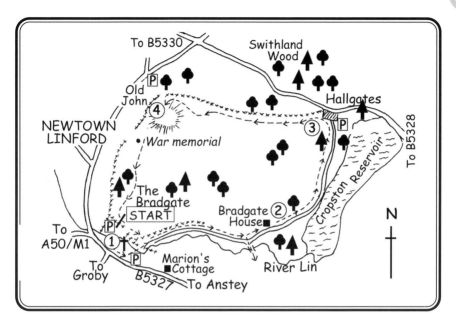

which it is supposed the bricks for the house were made. Return to the main path and you can have a closer look at **Bradgate House,** completed in 1502 for the Grey family. It is one of the earliest unfortified grand houses in England.

2 Follow the road alongside the Cropston Reservoir – part of the Victorian water supply scheme for Leicester and opened in 1870.

3 Just before you reach the **Hallgates carpark,** which is another entry/exit to **Bradgate,** go over to the crags at the edge of **Coppice Plantation.** Here you will see evidence of Charnwood's volcanic past. There are fine-grained rocks of volcanic dust cleaved and hardened into slates – looking zig-zagged in appearance. Now you should turn left round the plantation making for **Old John.** There are several routes possible and you can take your choice. However, if you bear left around **Sliding Stone Wood** you will, on your course there, pass through some of the original moorland of **Charnwood** – wet heath and bog. The crags in the wood indicate further volcanic material, this time agglomerates and solidified ash and dust heavily contorted and twisted.

④ Go on to **Old John,** a folly built in 1786, to commemorate an old retainer who was killed on the spot when a maypole fell on him at a coming of age party for the Earl of Stamford's relative. The beermug shape is alleged to reflect Old John's partiality for ale. Savour the view, and use the toposcope as this is the highest point in the park. Can you see Leicester? Belvoir Castle? Billesdon Coplow? Surely this outcrop will confirm the idea of Charnwood as a major volcanic area over 600 million years ago.

Consider too, from your viewpoint, that Bradgate was a medieval deer park and though much altered, even yet it conveys that sense of an ancient landscape. The danger today is that too many feet will erode pathways causing soil loss, and so careful management of the park is necessary so that the past can be conserved realistically, whilst allowing us to continue to enjoy it.

You can follow any route you choose back to the entrance but you might prefer to go past the war memorial then downhill to a clump of trees known as **Tyburn,** and thence to the car park. From there (don't forget **Marion s Cottage** to the left) turn right to return to the **Bradgate.**

PLACE OF INTEREST NEARBY

The Great Central Railway, Rothley, is approximately 3 miles to the east of Bradgate Park. It is Britain's only double track main line heritage railway. Steam train rides are available every weekend and bank holiday throughout the year and daily in the summer. Telephone: 01509 230726.

The Waterside Inn

THIS WALK WILL DELIGHT THOSE WHO LIKE TO RAMBLE AMONGST
THE INDUSTRIAL GRAVEYARDS OF ENGLAND. FIRST YOU SEE ONE
OF THE FINEST VIEWS IN THE MIDLANDS FROM THE CASTLE HILL.
THEN YOU PASS ONE OF THE LARGEST FORMER GRANITE QUARRIES
IN THE COUNTRY, NOW A LANDFILL SITE. THEN ACROSS THE COURSE
OF AN OLD RAILWAY AND SOON TO SWITHLAND RESERVOIR, BUILT
IN 1896 ALONG WITH SEVERAL OTHER 19TH-CENTURY RESERVOIRS
IN CHARNWOOD, TO SUPPLY LEICESTER. NEARBY YOU PASS
BUDDON WOOD, ONCE FOUGHT OVER BY ENVIRONMENTALISTS TO
SAVE IT FROM MINERAL EXPLOITATION BUT NOW ONE OF THE
BIGGEST 'HOLES' IN EUROPE.

There are some splendid walks around Mountsorrel, but, too often,
the floodwaters of the river Soar fill the intervening valley between

Sileby and Barrow on the far side and Mountsorrel on the other. Hence, this walk explores the firmer ground to the west of the village, which is compressed between the fine castle site and the river, now canalised as part of the Grand Union Canal. Along this route ran the Leicester to Derby road. For a great deal of time the village remained linear but has now expanded in its southern section towards Rothley Plain. The castle stood on granite or Mountsorrel Syenite as it is more properly known. This has been the key to the development of the village. Most buildings are constructed of it and so are the setts on the ground. The canal was the export point and at Jelly's Wharf it could be sent 'to any part of the Kingdom'. In this district were three almost indestructible materials: Mountsorrel granite, Swithland slate and Barrow lime mortar.

Also known as the Inn on the Lock, the **WATERSIDE INN** was built 200 years ago when the Grand Union Canal came through Loughborough to Leicester. It is situated next to the lock with the old humpback bridge close by and lots of canal traffic to watch from the beer garden and patio fronting onto the canal. This is a long building and the extension to the lounge took in the old stables where bargees kept their horses. Until 1965 the pub was known as the Duke of York. As you sit in the lounge not only do you have a fine view of the lock but also of the castle hill behind Mountsorrel. When you emerge at the rear you look across the flat valley of the river Soar towards Sileby, a village situated above the flood levels.

How to get there: Mountsorrel is 6 miles north of Leicester, very close to the A6. The nearest junction on the M1 is 23, then following the A512 and the A6.

Parking: There is a large car park at the Waterside Inn and a field next to the pub where you can leave your car while you walk, but beware the narrow road leading to it and the humpbacked bridge.

Length of the walk: 5 miles. Map: OS Landranger series 129 or OS Explorer 246 (GR 582152).

This is an Everards House with Everards Beacon, Tiger and Original cask ales plus a weekly guest cask. Lagers, ciders, wines, spirits and soft drinks are also available. Drinking times are 11.30 am to 2.30 pm and 6 pm to 11 pm Monday to Saturday and 12 noon to 3.30 pm Sundays (open all day Saturday and Sunday from Easter to September). The food is very good value and served most efficiently. The menu offers a selection of starters, main courses and desserts along with hot and cold snacks and a traditional roast on Sundays. Food is available every day from 12 noon to 2 pm and 6.30 pm to 9 pm (on Saturdays and Sundays food is available 12 noon to 8 pm from Easter to September). Smaller portions are available of some of the dishes at a reduced rate and during the winter months weekly specials are available. Children are welcome in the lower lounge area. Well-behaved dogs are allowed in the bar area.

✆ 0116 230 2758

THE WALK

1 From the **Waterside Inn** turn left and over the hump-backed bridge taking great care about the traffic here.

At the main road (once the A6, which now bypasses the town) turn left and cross into **Watling Street** on the opposite side. Go uphill noting the derelict buildings en route and also the profuse use of granite. Just before the road bears right go up some steps which lead to the castle hill. There are superb views all across the county from here. There may have been a Roman temple on this site and the Norman castle lasted until, by order of Henry III, it was destroyed because it was 'a nest of the devil and a den of thieves and robbers'. Return to the lane and carry on along it, passing Poplar House at the corner and bearing right. When you reach the T-junction go straight ahead into a trackway. You are still in an eminent position and can see the second of Mountsorrel's churches to your left. Note the large granite boulders along the edge of your track.

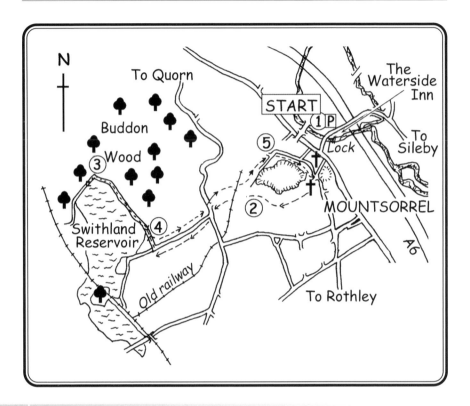

② As you bear right you are following round one of Britain's former largest quarries, now a landfill site. Keep away as it is dangerous, but, from time to time you do get glimpses of the rock face. Continue along the track until you reach a lane with a seat on the left. Here you turn left and cross an old railway bridge. The line formerly went south-west to join the Great Central Railway (now operated as a vintage steam railway). To your right is an area of scrub and bracken.

On reaching a more major road you see a sign opposite, 'Rushey Lane'. Cross over to this but turn left along the main road until you arrive at Kinchley Lane on the right in about 100 yards. Turn down this lane until you reach gates marking private land of the Severn-Trent Water Authority. Follow the road round to the right until you reach the Swithland Reservoir dam.

3 From this vantage point you can see the whole reservoir and, in the distance, the viaduct of the Great Central Railway.

4 We must, therefore, return by the same route. When you reach the junction of Kinchley Lane and the main road turn left and go about 100 yards to turn right into the lane from which you emerged earlier in the walk. Go down this lane but do not go back into your original track. Instead bear left and carry on until you reach the approach to the landfill site. Here there are several notices and white blocks to limit traffic, but you can walk through without any trouble. Thus you turn right through the approach road and go straight ahead until you see a tree-lined track in front. This also has two white stone blocks on it. Pass through and walk on until you reach the top end of Watling Street, close to your original start along the track. You should recognise this point. The castle hill is just ahead.

5 Turn left downhill until you are at the main village road, then turn left to reach the Sileby road in a short distance, on your right. This returns you to the Waterside Inn.

If you wish to shorten this walk you can complete the circle as the map shows without going on to Swithland Reservoir. This reduces the walk to 2 miles.

PLACE OF INTEREST NEARBY

In Bond Lane, Mountsorrel, is the **Stonehurst Family Farm & Motor Museum**. Here, you can see and touch friendly farmyard animals. Children can play in the straw barn and there is a large activity area. Free tractor and trailer rides are available, as well as pond dipping and pony rides. There is also an impressive collection of vintage cars and cycles to admire. A blacksmith's forge, farm shop, teashop and restaurant complete the scene. Telephone: 01509 413216.

The Belper Arms

THIS CIRCULAR WALK IS OVER FAIRLY LEVEL COUNTRYSIDE. A WIDE AND PLEASANT TRACK LEAVES THE VILLAGE HEADING SOUTH TO REACH AN OLD RAILWAY NEXT TO THE ASHBY CANAL. YOU CROSS THE LINE OF THE RAILWAY, NOW PLOUGHED OUT ON ONE SIDE. THEN YOU WALK ALONG THE CANAL TO SHACKERSTONE, WHICH MEANS THE VILLAGE OF THE ROBBERS. HERE THERE IS MUCH TO VIEW, NOT ONLY IN THE CHURCH AND VILLAGE, BUT ALSO THERE IS A FINE CASTLE SITE WHICH YOU SEE AS YOU CROSS BRIDGE 53. THE CANAL HAS A LOVELY BEND HERE WHICH IS MADE MORE ATTRACTIVE BY THE LONGBOATS MOORED ALONGSIDE. GO TO SHACKERSTONE RAILWAY STATION WHERE THERE IS A RAILWAY MUSEUM. BETWEEN EASTER AND THE END OF SEPTEMBER STEAM TRAINS RUN ON THE BATTLEFIELD LINE TO MARKET BOSWORTH AND TO THE BATTLEFIELD OF BOSWORTH, WHERE RICHARD III WAS

●●●

The sign on the **BELPER ARMS** proclaims that this is the oldest
pub in Leicestershire – 1290, but the outside setting is ordinary. It
is the inside which startles and delights the visitor, for surely this is
our dream pub realised. Low beams, nooks and crannies, pew-like
seats, antiques in themselves, chain-mail and shield on the walls,
many small plates which each have a special message, pewter, pots
– all these and more are contained in a twilight, cosy atmosphere
with roaring winter fires.

Then there is Uncle Fred or Five to Four Fred, the famous ghost.
He is mentioned in the *British Book of Ghosts* and his presence is
felt rather than seen. He does not like changes. When one landlord
attempted an alteration he found himself short of breath, another
was 'grabbed by the shoulder'. Fred likes women and seems to be
returning to find a lost love. Women have reported 'bottom
pinching' from out of thin air. Did he die in the old well reputed to
be beneath the pub? There are ancient deeds showing that the pub
was once called the Shepherd and Shepherdess but the name was
changed in 1876 when Lord Belper owned the village – what would
Fred think about that?

How to get there: Newton Burgoland is in north-west
Leicestershire and 6 miles away from Ibstock. Follow signs
from the A447 to Odstone. You can also approach from
junction 11 on the M42 via Appleby Magna and Snarestone
or from the A444 turning right at Twycross onto the B4116.
Parking: There is a large car park at the pub and next to the
main road. You can leave your car here if you prefer to take the
walk first and drink afterwards.
Length of the walk: 4 miles. Map: OS Landranger series 140 or
OS Explorer 232 (GR 370091).

This freehouse has Marston's Pedigree as well as changing guest beers and traditional ciders on draught. Drinking times are 12 noon to 3 pm and 6 pm to 11 pm Monday to Thursday; all day on Friday, Saturday and Sunday. There is a large garden at the rear with a children's adventure playground – plenty of room to run off excess energy. Children and dogs are welcome both inside and out, the latter on leads. There is a full menu available 12 noon to 2 pm and 6.30 pm to 9.30 pm weekdays; on Sundays there is a traditional roast with food also available between 7 pm and 9 pm. The normal full menu is versatile and varied using fresh, local produce, with game and fish dishes a speciality.

This is an outstanding pub and an exceptional walk which you must not miss!

✆ 01530 270530

THE WALK

① From the pub car park cross to the footpath sign opposite. Pass through a small estate of modern houses and near a lamp post you see the way through onto a lane. Turn left and go about 100 yards to a bend. Here go straight ahead between **Corner Farm** and **Drayton Fields Barn**. Soon you reach a junction where a path from the village joins the one you are on. Keep straight on and follow a clear and wide grassy track which can get very muddy at times.

You pass through rather unspectacular countryside, generally flat. You will see yellow marker posts and blue arrows along the route. After you have walked about 1 mile you come to a wooden handgate. Go through this and keep to the right-hand side of a large field. When you have crossed this field you arrive at a long straight lane running left to right in front of you. Cross straight over this, climb a small fence and go ahead for 100 yards to another tiny fence at the edge of a wood over the line of the old railway. In front of you see a spick and span sign pointing to Shackerstone.

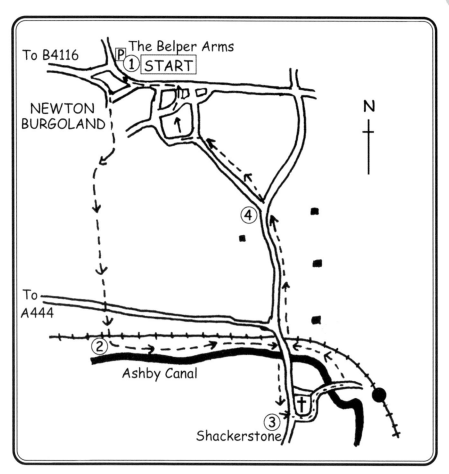

2 Now you are on the Ashby Canal towpath, at bridge 54. Turn left and follow the towpath to bridge 53 where a gate and stile take you onto the road. Turn right onto the bridge and look left for a good view of moored longboats and the castle site.

3 Carry on into the village. Turn left into Church Road and follow this round past the Rising Sun. Then turn right to cross a canal bridge and immediately left to walk on the towpath back to bridge 53. At this point you can divert to go to Shackerstone

railway station if you wish, returning to bridge 53 to continue the walk.

From bridge 53 ascend to the road and turn left, going over the old railway bridge where you will see below that this is now a road leading to the station car park. Walk along the country lane until you reach a Y fork in ½ mile.

4 Take the left fork and in another ½ mile, just before you reach Newton Burgoland, turn left into a narrow lane. On the right you see a footpath sign only 50 yards down the lane. Cross the stile here into the field towards the yellow marker post ahead. Go over another stile and follow a fenced path round to the village street. Turn right then left past the chapel (1807) into Dames Lane, then turn right to the main road. Here you turn left to return to the Belper Arms.

PLACES OF INTEREST NEARBY

Twycross Zoo is a few miles to the south on the A444. It is open daily except Christmas Day. Telephone: 01827 880250.

Some 4 miles to the north, near Coalville, is the **Snibston Discovery Park** where science, technology, history and art are on offer. The site also offers free entry to the foyer, shop, café and Grange Nature Reserve and Aboretum. Telephone: 01530 278444.